Worship and Sacrifice

by Thomas Westfield

with chapters by C. Matthew McMahon

Copyright Information

Worship and Sacrifice, by Thomas Westfield,
with chapters by C. Matthew McMahon, Ph.D., Th.D.
Edited by Therese B. McMahon

Published by Puritan Publications
A Ministry of A Puritan's Mind in Crossville, TN
www.apuritansmind.com
www.puritanpublications.com
www.reformedsynod.com
www.gracechapeltn.com

First Electronic Edition, 2026
First Modern Print Edition, 2026
Manufactured in the United States of America

eISBN: 978-1-62663-536-4
ISBN: 978-1-62663-537-1

Table of Contents

Introduction

By C. Matthew McMahon, Th.D., Ph.D.

"They made a calf in Horeb, and worshipped the molten image. Thus they changed their glory into the similitude of an ox that eateth grass," (Psalm 106:19–20).

What a verse! Here is the church of God trading glory for shame, the living God for a lump of metal, the Creator for a beast that feeds in the field. Psalm 106 is deafening in its point, a lightning strike against idolatry, unbelief, and the madness of worshipping anything less than God himself. Yet how many today are deaf to hear it, blind to see it, and hardened against its warning? People have no problem hanging up a "picture of Jesus" in their home and looking upon it with "high thoughts" "elevated thoughts". That's *worship*. It's idolatry. "There is no such thing as an innocent religious image."[1] And what then, shall be said about God's prescriptions in worship? Shall we do what God prescribes, or what we want to do? This is the heart of Psalm 106.

This little book you have before you gathers Thomas Westfield's burden for right worship in wrong times; in fact, two main ideas flow from his pen – worship and Christian sacrifice. The first 8 sermons deal with worship, then there are 2 sermons that deal with sacrifice, and then finally a sermon about honor and

---

[1] John Calvin (*Institutes* 2.8.17).

dishonor in the way ministers and Christians live in the world. His texts are simple and sharp. From Psalm 106 he shows what false worship looks like when a people *forgets God*: a golden image, a stiff neck, and a settled refusal to trust the voice of the Lord. From Hebrews 13 he shows what true worship in *sacrifice* looks like now that Christ has come: not bulls and goats, but spiritual sacrifices—praise with the lips, mercy with the hands, and contentment in the heart—offered "by him," and so accepted by God. And then he closes in his last sermon by reminding ministers and congregations alike that the same Christ who receives our sacrifices also leads us through seasons of honor and dishonor, good report and evil report, where the test is not whether we are liked, but whether we remain *faithful*.

Westfield's reading of Psalm 106 comes with a pastor's edge. Israel's sin at Horeb was not mere error; it was exchange. "Thus they changed their glory into the similitude of an ox that eateth grass," (Psalm 106:20). They did not only bow to a wrong object; they traded away the living God for something that could be forged, carried, and then carried off. Later, at the border of promise, the same spirit took a subtler shape. It sounded like sober realism and prudent caution. But the inspired verdict is plainer: "Yea, they despised the pleasant land, they believed not his word: But murmured in their tents, and hearkened not unto the voice of the LORD," (Psalm 106:24–25).

Isn't that the anatomy of *false worship*? Idolatry, unbelief, and murmuring are not three separate vices sprinkled at random through the wilderness narrative; they are one braided cord. When the heart no longer fears and loves God, it must invent a *safer god*—one that will bless our desires and never cross them. When that false god cannot carry the weight of real life, the heart turns sour and begins to mutter at the real God: his timing is wrong, his providence is unkind, his commands are hard, his promises are thin. What begins at the altar shows up around the dinner table. What we *adore* determines how we *live*, and how we live unavoidably exposes what—or whom—we truly adore (*i.e.* worship and sacrifice). "Neither murmur ye, as some of them also murmured, and were destroyed of the destroyer," (1 Corinthians 10:10).

Westfield will not let us keep that narrative at a safe distance. He presses the contrast with our own land and our own lives. Israel despised the gift of a rich land after years of bondage; we risk despising the Lord's gifts after years of plenty. They preferred the certainty of Egypt's chains to the *risks* of faith. We can prefer the safety of our comforts to the obedience of faith. They murmured "in their tents"; we murmur in our homes, our pews, and under our breath. For Westfield, the issue is *worship*: whom we trust, how we speak of him, and whether we will obey his voice when obedience costs us.

From that ground the sermons turn to Hebrews 13 and answers the obvious question: What worship will God now accept in the lives of his people in sacrifice to him? Will New Testament Christians offer sacrifice still? What does holy adoration of the living God put in motion look like? The old covenant altars have fallen silent because the once-for-all sacrifice in Christ has been offered. "By him therefore let us offer the sacrifice of praise to God continually," (Hebrews 13:15). The form has changed, but not the *seriousness*. The same God who rejected the golden calf and judged a faithless generation has told us through his apostles what pleases him now. Where do people like to often look? "Thus, they erred, who sought Christ and his apostles not in the sacred writings, but on painted walls."[2] They like pictures and bumper stickers and call it "holiness." But Westfield turns our attention *to the way we live*. The way we worship always points us in a specific direction.

Westfield gathers Hebrews' strands and clasps them under three ideas—praise, mercy, joy—and insists that each is a real sacrifice, and each must come "by him" to God. The center is Christ's priesthood. We can only offer what God will accept if it is offered through the Son he gave for us and by the Spirit he has given to us. How do we live in this way? What do we do? What are our "sacrifices" to God?

First, praise. "The fruit of our lips giving thanks to his name," (Hebrews 13:15). For Westfield, this is not a call to chase a mood or to perform an hour of decency

---

[2] Augustine, The Harmony of the Gospels, 1.10 [NPNF1, 6:83; PL 34.1049].

before we hurry back to the week that really matters. He means a God-ward life with a God-ward mouth. He quotes David: "Let my prayer be set forth before thee as incense; and the lifting up of my hands as the evening sacrifice," (Psalm 141:2). Again: "The sacrifices of God are a broken spirit: a broken and a contrite heart, O God, thou wilt not despise," (Psalm 51:17). And he draws in Paul: "I beseech you therefore, brethren... present your bodies a living sacrifice, holy, acceptable unto God, which is your reasonable service," (Romans 12:1). In other words, praise is not a thin veneer of holy words; it is the whole person—mind, tongue, and body—turned God-ward because Christ has brought us near.

Second, mercy. "But to do good and to communicate forget not: for with such sacrifices God is well pleased," (Hebrews 13:16) Westfield labors here, because many of us *sing* better than we *testify* or *share*. He refuses to narrow "communicate" to money only, though he won't let the rich off the hook. He urges the people to do good to the public by strengthening the places where worship and wisdom grow; to do good to the private by touching both soul and body—teaching the ignorant, directing the confused, restoring the fallen, admonishing the unruly, comforting the cast-down, praying for the helpless; defending the weak, lending to the needy, and giving, not with grudging words, but with cheerful faces and swift hands. He is very plain that the gift must be ours to give—no stolen sacrifices—and very plain that the gift must spring from compassion, not vanity. He quotes the Lord: "Lend, hoping for nothing again," (Luke 6:35) He quotes the Psalmist: "He hath dispersed, he hath given to the poor; his righteousness endureth for ever," (Psalm 112:9). He quotes the apostle's promise: "God loveth a cheerful giver," (2 Corinthians 9:7).

Third, joy in this work. Westfield refuses to treat this as a *hobby virtue*. He calls it an *act of worship* rooted in promise. "Let your conversation be without covetousness; and be content with such things as ye have." Why? "For he hath said, I will never leave thee, nor forsake thee," (Hebrews 13:5). He lingers over that pledge, reminding hearers that in Greek the sentence piles up negatives for emphasis—God's way of binding up our fearful hearts. Faith receives that word, walks in honest callings, and refuses to grasp at gain through trickery, false measure, or restless worry. Murmuring melts when the promise is believed.

Westfield then sets embers in the pastoral hearth by reminding us that acceptable worship in sacrifice of our lives must be offered by acceptable people. Abel is received, then his offering; Cain is not received, *therefore* his offering is not received. We are not accepted because our worship is flawless; our right worship is accepted because our persons are received *in the Beloved*. This is the same as when we do any good works outside of the corporate church setting. The stain that clings even to holy things is borne by our High Priest, so that our *broken hallelujahs* please God for Christ's sake. But that truth does not excuse carelessness; it gives the courage to *obey* with zeal. By him we draw near; by him we offer; by him we persist. "That we shall...endeavour...the reformation of religion in the kingdoms of England and Ireland, in doctrine, worship , discipline, and government, according to the word of God, and example of the best reformed churches."[3] In all our good works we strive for this reformation in religion and blessing to our neighbor.

The final sermon, taken from 2 Corinthians 6:8, supplies a sober frame for all of this. Those who worship God as he commands will *not* always be praised for it. There will be seasons "by honour and dishonour, by evil report and good report: as deceivers, and yet true," (2 Corinthians 6:8). Westfield recounts how even the Lord Jesus rode in to cries of "Hosanna" and walked out to cries of "Crucify," how Paul could be treated as a god at Lystra and stoned like a dog the same day. The point is not grim romance. The point is steadiness. Acceptable worship is not fragile; it does not wilt when the wind shifts. The same Lord who says, "With such sacrifices God is well pleased," also says, "Blessed are ye, when men shall revile you... for my sake," (Matthew 5:11). The call is to hold the course—speak the truth, offer the sacrifices of praise and mercy, keep a clean conscience, and leave our name with God. "I have fought a good fight, I have finished my course, I have kept the faith," (2 Timothy 4:7).

---

3 *Solemn League and Covenant* of the 1647 Westminster Standards.

What, then, is Westfield saying to our day in all these works? To sum up, that the worship *God accepts* (both in corporate worship and out of church in daily living) is not vague sincerity, not aesthetic uplift, not the sum of our preferences, but Christ-centered obedience expressed in praise, mercy, and joy with what He's given. That God still refuses the worship that swaps his glory for manageable idols, the worship that will not trust his promises, the worship that murmurs in the tent after singing in the court. That ministers and lay people alike must brace themselves to persevere when honor turns to dishonor, and good report to evil in daily sacrifice of what God expects form us.

It's hard not to give a brief word to the Evangelical church that *shrugs* at proper worship and sacrifice in life. The church is rich in worldly resources and poor in godly reverence. They are strong on the parts of invented "worship" they like and wicked on the parts God commands; and that is always seen in the way they act outside the church. People have learned to prize gifted leaders more than faithful pastors; production more than prayer; breadth more than holiness; novelty more than obedience. They can fill a room with sound and leave God's poor unfed, our neighbors untaught, and our hearts unchanged. They can talk for hours about the culture and give minutes *to true confession.* They can soothe covetousness by calling it ambition, and justify murmuring by calling it authenticity.

If Westfield stood among us, I think he would ask two plain questions. First, are we worshiping the God who is, *or the god we wish we had*? The test is not our mood but our obedience. "Yea, they despised the pleasant land, they believed not his word: But murmured in their tents," (Psalm 106:24–25) Second, are we bringing the sacrifices God names in holiness? "By him therefore let us offer the sacrifice of praise to God continually... But to do good and to communicate forget not: for with such sacrifices God is well pleased," (Hebrews 13:15–16) Praise without mercy is noise. Mercy without praise is philanthropy. Contentment without either is stoicism. The Lord wants all three, offered through his Son.

This is not a call to *earn* favor. It is a call to live as those who already have it. The Father who did not spare his own Son has brought us near so that we might speak well of his Name, open our hands to his image-bearers, and rest our anxious souls on his promise. He has told us what he will *accept*, and he has given us the Priest by whom he accepts it.

So, take up this book as a mirror and a goad. Let Psalm 106 show you where worship goes wrong. Let Hebrews 13 show you what sacrificial worship God now accepts in your life. And let 2 Corinthians 6 cause you to stand strong for the seasons when pleasing God will displease men. Then, by him, offer your sacrifices—not once, but continually—and know that your Father sees, receives, and delights. "I will never leave thee, nor forsake thee," (Hebrews 13:5).

In Christ's grace and mercy,
C. Matthew McMahon, Ph.D., Th.D.
From My study, September, 2025
"...search the Scriptures..." (John 5:39).
www.apuritansmind.com
www.puritanpublications.com
www.gracechapeltn.com
www.reformedsynod.com

Meet Thomas Westfield

By C. Matthew McMahon, Th.D., Ph.D.

Thomas Westfield (1573-1644), later Bishop of Bristol and member of the Westminster Assembly, was born in Ely in 1573. Schooled first at St. Mary's under Master Spight, he went on to Jesus College, Cambridge, where he advanced quickly in learning, securing a fellowship and taking his degrees with steady diligence: B.A. in 1593, M.A. in 1596, Bachelor of Divinity in 1604, and Doctor of Divinity in 1615. He was also incorporated at Oxford, and even admitted to Gray's Inn, marking him as a man both studious and capable in ecclesiastical and civil affairs.

His early ministry was spent under Nicholas Felton at St. Mary-le-Bow, and from there he moved into the settled course of parish life. He first held the rectory of South Somercotes in Lincolnshire, then exchanged it for the city charge of St. Bartholomew's, Smithfield in 1605. Later he took up the rectory of Hornsey (1615–1637) and was made prebendary of St. Paul's. His diligence and fidelity commended him to further preferment: Archdeacon of St. Albans in 1631, and two years later appointed to a royal commission to oversee ecclesiastical jurisdiction.

When the storms of civil war broke over England, Westfield found himself caught in the crosswinds of suspicion. Though long a London minister, he was reproached as a royalist and treated with contempt in the streets, even sequestered from his pulpit at St. Bartholomew's. In 1642 he fled to the king and was consecrated Bishop of Bristol, a charge once offered him in his youth but declined until later years, when he had means to sustain the dignity of the office with his own hospitality. Even then, his revenues were withheld by Parliament, though later restored to him out of respect for his character. He was invited to the Westminster Assembly, and though his part in its debates was modest, he was present at its first gathering in July 1643.

Westfield's ministry was marked not by polemical heat but by a tenderness of spirit that moved many. So deep was his pathos in the pulpit that he was known as the "weeping prophet." Once, preaching before the king at Oxford, his nerves so overcame him that he fainted. Yet in ordinary course, his tears and trembling only added force to his appeals, as he labored to press sin upon the conscience and Christ upon the heart.

He authored collections of sermons, including *England's Face in Israel's Glass* (1646), which set the sins and mercies of the nation in the mirror of God's dealings with his ancient people, and *The White Robe, or the Surplice Vindicated* (1660), a defense of the Church's use of vestments. After his death, further sermons were gathered and published as *Eleven Choice Sermons* (1656: now republished in this volume).

Westfield died in 1644 and was buried in the choir of Bristol Cathedral. His wife, Elizabeth Meetkirk, erected a monument in his memory. He left behind her and a daughter, also named Elizabeth.

Westfield's life was one of contrasts—honour and dishonour, good report and evil report—yet he held his ministry with faithfulness to the end. His name belongs among those divines who, though buffeted by the tumults of their age, sought above all to see that God's worship be rightly offered, and that his people be taught to offer sacrifices with which he is well pleased.

For further study:

[Cole's Collections in Brit. Mus. Addit. MSS. 5811 ff. 78-9, 5820 f. 152; Wood's Fasti Oxon. ed. Bliss, i. 345, ii. 70; Walker's Sufferings of the Clergy, 1714, ii. 3; Lloyd's Memoires, 1668, pp. 300-5; Newcourt's Repert. Londin. i. 95, 128, 296, 653; Le Neve's Fasti Eccles. Anglicanae; Lansdowne MS. 985, f. 62; Foster's Alumni Oxon. 1500-1714; Fuller's Worthies of England, 1811, i. 160; Hennessy's Novum Repert. Eccles. Londin. 1898, pp. 18, 27, 101, 223; Harl. MS. 7176, pp. 172-5; Hetherington's Hist. of the Westminster Assembly, 1878, pp. 105, 113.]

To the Reader

Man is very inclined to evil, having within him a fountain of natural corruption. When this is drawn out by example, the stream runs even more violently. All the kings of Israel, as far as I can read, were bad enough. Yet many of them are especially marked with infamy for this particular sin: their imitation of Jeroboam the son of Nebat.

It has often been said that this nation of ours is quick to imitate others. And it is to be feared that, together with their foreign foolishness, we also share in many of their gross sins. Certainly, the likeness between Israel and England holds true, as the following discourse will show. Our mercies have been in no way inferior to theirs. Our sins, if not greater, have at least run parallel with theirs. And as for our miseries, sad experience speaks more loudly than any silent witness.

The earlier subject of this book, though it is mostly sorrowful—treating of sins and judgments—yet the wisdom and sweetness of the reverend author has, like Samson, brought honey out of the lion.

As for the latter part, concerning sharing with the needs of the saints, the practice of this worthy man was itself a pattern worthy of admiration.

Most of these sermons were preached at Highgate, which was indeed highly exalted by the diligent preaching of this minister of Christ. And I wish that neither our Savior's prediction concerning

Capernaum, nor David's wish regarding the mountains of Gilboa, may ever spiritually or literally fall upon it.

And you, West Smithfield, that were watered for so long with the heavenly drops of this worthy Westfield—as once you were with the blood of many courageous martyrs who weekly suffered within you—having been thus honored, do not become like the beasts within you that perish.

And if there are any who had relation to him, who, like wanton children, wasted away the time while this shining torch was burning and giving light, let them at least now make use of this last inch of light. With God's blessing, it may gain them treasure for eternity.

In honor of his memory, and for the benefit of all who will make use of this help, I have raised up this pillar of his own upon his grave. By this, and other such means, may both you and I be edified. This is the desire of,

T.S.

Sermon 1

Psalm 106:19–20, etc. "They made a calf in Horeb, and worshipped the molten image. Thus they changed their glory into the similitude of an ox, etc."

In this psalm you have many of the sins of this people recorded. In the three former verses there is the mutiny of Korah and Abiram against Moses, and of two hundred and fifty men with Korah; they envied Aaron, the saint of God.

In these verses you have another sin of this people, a fearful one: the sin of idolatry.

There are some sins of the highest nature. Such we reckon those sins that are directly against God—atheism, profanity, idolatry, and the like.

There are some sins directly against nature—such as sodomy, bestiality, incestuous defilement, and so forth.

Some are directly against human society—such as rapes, murder, oppression, and the shedding of innocent blood. Now idolatry belongs to the first kind, and it is the worst. Tertullian, I think most excellently, says that idolatry contains under it *omnes species peccati* (all kinds of sin). There is treason in idolatry: the idolater sets up a new god, as the traitor sets up a new king. There is falsehood and lying in idolatry, for an idol is "the teacher of lies" (Habakkuk 2:18). There is theft in it, for what greater robbery can there be than to rob God of His glory? There is whoredom in it; it is often in Scripture called by that name, for it is spiritual whoredom. How often do I read the phrase of men going a whoring after another god?

Now, mark the text and observe three things *here:*

First, the idol after which they went a whoring. It is called in the first verse of my text *a calf*. In the second verse it is called *an ox*. A young ox, a young bullock, a young heifer of three years old I have observed in Scripture to be called by the name of a calf. And it was not a living calf or a living bullock, but in the former verse it is called the molten image of a calf. In the second verse, the likeness of an ox. That was their idol.

Secondly, consider the work of this people about that idol—their sin, in three things: First, they made it: "They made a calf in Horeb." Secondly, they worshipped it: "They worshipped the molten image."

Thirdly, "They changed their glory into the likeness of it."

Then mark further the cause of this sin, the root from which it sprang. It arose from forgetfulness of God, the God who was their Savior. "They forgat God their Saviour," (Psalm 106:21). And then from forgetfulness of His works. These were:

First, *magna*—great works. Then *mirabilia*—wondrous works. And then *terribilia*—terrible works. "They forgat God their Saviour, which had done great things in Egypt; wondrous works in the land of Ham, and terrible things by the Red sea," (Psalm 106:21–22). This is the *sum* of the whole text. I may not think to go over all these at one time, for it is a matter that cannot easily be passed over. There are a generation of men that will compass sea and land to win us to idolatry; it would be good for our hearts to be established against it. I will go as far as the time will allow.

I begin first with the idol. It was a calf, or a young bullock.

God forbids *any* image to be made for *use* in religion, of anything in heaven above, or in the earth beneath, or in the waters under the earth (*see his commandments*). God specifies all these places because there is none of them—neither heaven above, nor earth beneath, nor waters under the earth—but that the foolish, vain heart of man has found out something there to deify, to make *into* a god.

Some have worshipped the sun, moon, and stars, the host of heaven—glorious creatures, yet such creatures as God made to serve man, and not man to serve them. Some of the Gentiles worshipped men like themselves. Some worshipped four-footed beasts. Some creeping things of the earth. That idol Dagon, which you read of in Scripture, had the head of a man but the lower parts of it were like a fish. Not to weary you with a long account of particular vanities in this kind, hear what the Apostle says of the Gentiles: "Because that, when they knew God, they glorified him not as God, neither were thankful; but became vain in their imaginations, and their foolish heart was darkened. Professing themselves to be wise, they became fools, And changed the glory of the uncorruptible God into an image made like to corruptible man, and to birds, and fourfooted beasts, and creeping things. Wherefore God also gave them up to uncleanness through the lusts of their own hearts, to dishonour their own bodies between themselves: Who changed the truth of God into a lie, and worshipped and served the creature more than the Creator, who is blessed for ever. Amen," (Romans 1:21–25).

A question may be raised here: why did this people, since they insisted on worshipping God under a form, choose this *particular* form? Why a calf? Why a young bullock?

It is agreed by both ancient and modern writers that they learned this form of service in Egypt. Egypt was the *mother of idolatry*, as Jeremiah calls it. Though all people under heaven had corrupted their ways, yet no people had more corrupted their ways in this regard than Egypt. *Quis nescit qualia demens Aegyptus?* (Who does not know what base abominations foolish Egypt practiced?) What vile and shameful gods did the Egyptians worship! They worshipped a deity under the form of a crocodile. Another deity under the form of an *ichneumon*, a kind of rat of the Nile. Another under the form of an *ibis*. And they had even more worthless gods than these—even their onions and leeks in their gardens. *O sanctus, etc.* The heathen themselves mocked this foolishness, that they should have deities growing in their gardens. But of all the gods they worshipped, the greatest, their chief god, was Apis, or Serapis. They worshipped him under the likeness or form of a young bullock—a piebald bull, a piebald ox, black with certain white spots upon him.

Would you know from where this came? Let me detain you for a while. Apis, a king from another country, during a famine relieved Egypt, especially Alexandria. When he was dead, they made him into a god and decreed that divine honor should be given him. Then they must worship him under a form. They remembered the benefit they had by Apis. They had their grain by the tillage of the ground, by the labor of the ox. And so they would worship this great god of theirs under the form of a piebald ox, a young piebald bullock.

This people had seen this idolatrous service in Egypt, and now they longed not only after Egyptian food, but also after this Egyptian god.

Mark what Stephen says of this people in Acts 7:39: "To whom our fathers would not obey, but thrust him from them, and in their hearts turned back again into Egypt," (Acts 7:39). Saying, "Make us a calf, make us gods to go before us." In their hearts they turned back into Egypt when they required such worship of Aaron.

The thing I observe from this is:

Observation. It is an easy matter for men to be drawn into the practice of that idolatry which they have been accustomed to see in those places where they have long lived.

He that would guard himself against idolatry must beware of Egypt. The very air of Egypt (if I may say so) is infectious in this regard. See here: they had seen the worship of a young bullock in Egypt, and now they must have a bullock. Remember Jeroboam the son of Nebat, who made Israel to sin. How did he make them sin? He set up two calves. They set up one; he set up two—one at Dan, another at Bethel. Where did he learn that? Had he been in Egypt too? Yes, he lived in Egypt for a time. He fled there for fear of Solomon. For when he perceived that Solomon sought his life, he went and dwelt with Shishak, king of Egypt, and remained with him, as the text says, until the death of Solomon (1 Kings 11:40). I say, he that would take heed of idolatry, let him take heed how he dwells in Egypt.

The local seat of Antichrist (and what seat can that be but Rome?) is called in the Revelation by three names. It is called Egypt (Revelation 11:8). It is called Sodom in the same verse. It is called Babylon in many places in Revelation. It is called Babylon in regard to her cruelty. It is called Sodom, in regard to her filthiness. And it is called Egypt in regard to her idolatry.

It is a hard matter for a man to live in Egypt and not taste or savor somewhat of the idolatry of Egypt. We once had in England a proverb about going to Rome: They said, the first time a man went to Rome, he went to see a wicked man there. The second time he went to

Rome, he went to be acquainted with that wicked man there. The third time he went, he brought him home with him. How many have we seen (and it is a pity to see so many) of our nobility and gentry go to those Egyptian parts, and return home again—yet few of them bring home the same manners, the same religion, or the same souls they carried out with them.

Isaac bestowed the blessing upon Jacob, his younger son—you know the narrative in Genesis 27. But when Isaac sent his son Jacob to Padan-aram, though he had blessed him before, the Scripture says he blessed him again (Genesis 28:1). If ever parents had need to bless their children, they have need to bless them, and bless them again, when they send them to travel into those foreign parts. Can a man be in a mill where much grain is ground and not carry away some dust upon his clothes? Can liquor be stored in a musty vessel and not taste of the cask? Can a man live in Ethiopia and his face not be tanned? Mark in verse 35 of this psalm I now have in hand: it is said, "But were mingled among the heathen, and learned their works," (Psalm 106:35). It is a hard matter for a man to be much *among idolaters* and not *learn* idolatry. It is a hard matter for a man to keep company with drunkards and not learn to drink. It is a hard matter for a man to be a common companion with those that sit in the seat of the scornful and not learn to scoff. It is a hard matter for a man to live among blasphemers and swearers and not learn to swear. "Woe is me, that I sojourn in Mesech, that I dwell in the tents of Kedar!"

(Psalm 120:5). Brethren, if by any means, through prayer or all holy endeavors, you can keep yourselves from the woe of living in Mesech among idolaters, strive to do it. It is a miserable condition to live among idolatrous or wicked persons.

But if divine providence shall necessarily cast you into Mesech and Egypt; if it stands with the good will and pleasure of God, and there is no remedy but that the cords of your tents must be fastened among the tents of Kedar, among idolaters—then learn and remember how Noah lived in the old world: he walked with God when all the world walked away from Him. Remember how Lot lived in Sodom, how Joseph lived in Pharaoh's court, and Obadiah in Ahab's court, and Daniel in Babylon's court. Remember how the saints lived in Nero's household (Philippians 4:22). Remember a church that held fast the name of God and did not deny the faith, though they lived in the place where Satan's throne was (Revelation 2:13). The fish keeps its fresh taste though it lives in salt water. A myrtle does not lose its nature; it is still a myrtle though it grows in the midst of nettles.

It is a great shame to live among good men, in good places, and not be good. But it is a high commendation to live among evil men, in evil places, and not be evil. In this way much shall suffice concerning the idol: it was a calf, and they learned to make it in Egypt.

I come now to their work, the *making* of it. "They made a calf in Horeb." There are three circumstances in that making of it.

First, who were they that made it? They made it. Secondly, where did they make it? In Horeb. Thirdly, of what did they make it? That my text does not speak of here, but we must gather it from the narrative. It was of the golden earrings that Aaron took out of the ears of the men and women, of their sons and daughters, and from that they made a calf. "They made a calf in Horeb."

For the first, the people that made it: *They* made it. The Hebrews, the Jews, would gladly put this away from themselves. They say that there were some Egyptians mingled among them; and indeed, we read that there came out of Egypt a great mixed multitude, a confused company. But it was not these only that made the calf. The Israelites themselves made it too: "They made it." Yet I do not think that all of them had a hand in making it. Without question, some of them hated this calf with a perfect hatred, and hated those that made it, and those that worshipped it. It was only some of the people that made it. Hear what the Apostle says: "Neither be ye idolaters, as were *some* of them; as it is written, The people sat down to eat and drink, and rose up to play," (1 Corinthians 10:7). But some of them were idolaters—yes, a great company of them were idolaters. They made the calf.

But how can it be said, "They made it"? For if you look at the narrative, you will find that Aaron made it. Aaron threw their gold into the furnace. Aaron polished the calf. Aaron set up an altar. Aaron proclaimed a holy day: "Tomorrow is a feast to the Lord." It was Aaron that made it. Why then is it not said that Aaron made the calf in Horeb, but rather, "They made the calf"?

Mark the words where this narrative is set down, Exodus 32:35: "And the LORD plagued the people, because they made the calf, which Aaron made," (Exodus 32:35). Mark that well: God plagued the people for their sin in making the calf which Aaron made. So, the people and Aaron *both* made it: the people first—"They made it." Take these rules:

A man may have a hand, he may have fellowship in the unfruitful works of darkness, in many ways—four especially.

It is the usual phrase of Scripture:

1. A man is said to do that which he does not himself, but another does, if he commands it. That is one way. So, David slew Uriah the Hittite with the sword, because he commanded him to be set in the front of the battle where he might be slain with the sword of the children of Ammon (2 Samuel 11:15–17).
2. A man may be said to do that which another man does, if he counsels, persuades, entices, or urges him to it. Thus the high priests and the scribes and Pharisees are said, with their wicked hands,

to have taken Christ and crucified Him and slain Him. They with their own hands did not do it, but they persuaded Pilate to do it with much importunity; therefore they did it (Acts 2:23).

3. A man may be said to do that which another does if he occasions the doing of it. It is said of Judas, that he purchased a field (Acts 1:18). This man purchased a field. Judas did not purchase it, but by returning the money to the treasury again for which he sold Christ, he gave them occasion to purchase it. Therefore, this man purchased the field.
4. A man may be said to do that which another does if he does not hinder the doing of it when he ought and might have hindered it. The men of Tyre came upon the Sabbath day and sold wares in Jerusalem. Nehemiah, that good governor, went to the rulers of the people and said, "What evil thing is this that ye do, and profane the sabbath day?" (Nehemiah 13:17). They broke it, because they should have hindered the breaking of it and did not.

We have sins enough, and too many of our own, to answer for. We need not answer for the sins of others. Yet we shall answer for the sins of others too—all those sins that other men commit—if either we,

- Command them.
- Counsel them.

- Occasion them.
- Or do not hinder them.

Aaron made the calf, but yet *they* made it, because *they wanted him to make it.*

Aaron made it. And this must be considered a little. Did Aaron sin in making this calf, or not? Did Aaron do well in yielding to the people in making this calf? *Tantum sacerdotem condemnare non audemus, et excusare non possumus* (We dare not condemn so great a high priest, and yet we cannot excuse him), says Ambrose. Yet some in former times, and one in later days among us (but a Papist), Munsius, wrote a book *De Aarone Purgato* ("Of Aaron Purged"). He would free Aaron from all manner of sin in making this calf. But it will not do. Should he purge him with nitre and with fullers' soap seven times over, he could not do it. I see the Fathers are very careful in softening this sin; and we may lessen it, but excuse it, *we cannot.* We must acknowledge it as a very great sin in this high priest.

First of all, they say, the people would have him do it. He would not have done it otherwise.

Well, be it so. He was now a governor left under Moses. He should have been more watchful and looked better to his government. The permission of an evil is as great an evil as the commission of it. Woe to that people who are indulged in their sins either by their *ministers* or by their *magistrates.* The one ought to rebuke them, the other ought to punish them. But woe to the people who are indulged in their sins.

But then you will say, this people was set upon mischief; they would have it, there would be no remedy. Indeed, Aaron told Moses so.

It is true, they were so. Be it so. Yet Aaron should have been more vigilant, more courageous, more resolute in his government to withstand them.

But they were urgent and clamorous; they would never leave off pressing Aaron until he had done it.

Be it so: yet this importunity of theirs, though it may lessen the fault, cannot excuse it. Or, if you will say it may excuse it, it can only excuse it *à tanto* (in part), but not *à toto* (altogether); it may qualify it somewhat, but it cannot justify it.

But, they say, it is likely the people would have stoned him if he had not done it.

It is likely enough; they were ready enough to take up stones, for they did so to Moses. But grant it were so—Aaron should have chosen rather to have died a thousand deaths than to suffer the Almighty God to be so dishonored. We know what some said afterward in the like case: "Be it known unto thee, O king, that we will not serve thy gods, nor worship the golden image which thou hast set up. Our God whom we serve is able to deliver us from the burning fiery furnace, and he will deliver us out of thine hand, O king. But if not, be it known unto thee, O king, that we will not serve thy gods," (Daniel 3:17–18).

There is no question, Aaron cannot be excused in this sin. You may truly say in this way so far for Aaron:

that what he did, he did out of fear, and out of weakness, and out of cowardice. He did not dare displease the people; he did it out of fear and frailty. But take the sin in itself—oh, it is a dreadful sin in its own nature. Look in Deuteronomy 9:20, and you shall find what Moses says concerning it: "And the LORD was very angry with Aaron to have destroyed him: and I prayed for Aaron also the same time," (Deuteronomy 9:20). *Note* that well. God was angry with Aaron for this sin—very angry with him, so angry that He would have destroyed him, had not Moses made intercession for him. Now the anger of God does not usually break forth like fire upon His servants except for mighty provocations. Surely God was *greatly* provoked against Aaron, that He would have destroyed him, had not Moses interceded. There is no excusing it.

But then—this is a point of use, and I must not pass it by—why did not God so establish this His servant that he might not fall into such a sin as this? The Apostle says, "But the Lord is faithful, who shall stablish you, and keep you from evil," (2 Thessalonians 3:3). Again, Paul assures himself: "And the Lord shall deliver me from every evil work, and will preserve me unto his heavenly kingdom," (2 Timothy 4:18). God was able to establish Aaron so that he should not have yielded, out of weakness, to their request.

It is true. But it pleased God to leave Aaron to himself; He *allowed* him to fall. And you may well think that God had some good ends in it. God, being good, would not allow evil to be in the world unless He knew how to order that evil toward some greater good. Surely, there was some special purpose why God permitted Aaron to fall into such a dreadful sin as this. I will tell you what I conceive.

The first was this: to show that the Levitical priesthood of the old law was imperfect. How could the priest of the old law perfectly reconcile a poor sinner to God, since he himself was a sinner? Look in Hebrews 7, and you shall see the Apostle there shows the difference between our Lord Jesus Christ, the High Priest of the New Testament, and the priests of the Old Testament. Verse 27 says: "Who needeth not daily, as those high priests, to offer up sacrifice, first for his own sins, and then for the people's: for this he did once, when he offered up himself," (Hebrews 7:27). The priest of the old law was not only to offer for the sins of the people, but for his own sins—yes, first for his own sins, and then for the sins of the people. Now, how shall one sinner reconcile another sinner to God? *It cannot be.* Therefore, the Apostle says in verse 26: "For such an high priest became us, who is holy, harmless, undefiled, separate from sinners, and made higher than the heavens," (Hebrews 7:26). That is one reason: to show that the priesthood of the old law could not perfectly reconcile men to God.

A second reason why God permitted Aaron to fall was this: that, in so great a dignity as Aaron was now placed, in so high a calling as the high priesthood, he might learn to walk humbly with his God. Nothing so beats down a child of God in his own eyes as the sight of his own corruption and the sense of his own unworthiness. Solomon tells us that all the afflictions that God sends a man under the sun are to humble him (Ecclesiastes 1:13). And even that is too little. God is often forced to let loose the corruptions of His children, to suffer them to endure fearful conflicts, to feel the buffeting of Satan, a thorn in the flesh to trouble them. He lets them taste many fearful trials in the flesh, so that, finding such a Jebusite in the land, such an enemy in their own bosoms, such a thorn in their eyes and prick in their sides, the proud heart may never find time to sit down and bless itself in any gift or grace with which God has honored it.

No, this is not all. God does not only allow corruptions to grow in His children, that He may humble them, but He sometimes allows His children to fall into some great sin so that they may not fall into pride. Augustine says this, and I am bold to repeat it: I think it is sometimes profitable for the children of God to sin, to keep them from falling into pride. Just as a physician, when he would cure a convulsion, may work to bring on a fever; so God, to cure pride—that dangerous sin in His children—often suffers them to fall into other sins, though dreadful in themselves, that they may not fall into pride.

When men grow proud of any gift or grace that God has given them, then, as Gregory says, they make a sore out of a salve. Therefore, God lets them fall into other sins, that He may make a salve out of a sore—that when a man has been wounded by his own virtues, he may be healed by his own vices. That is the second reason.

Thirdly, I believe God permitted Aaron to fall for this reason: to teach him, as a priest, to look compassionately upon poor sinners, considering himself. Remember the Apostle's precept in Galatians 6:1, "Brethren, if a man be overtaken in a fault, ye which are spiritual, restore such an one in the spirit of meekness; considering thyself, lest thou also be tempted." Restore him again—the Greek word means, set him in joint again. Do you see him out of joint? Handle him gently, as you would set a dislocated bone—set him in joint again with the spirit of meekness. Why? "Considering thyself, lest thou also be tempted." That good father, when he heard of his brother's fall, cried out, "Alas! he fell today, and I may fall tomorrow." O consider yourself. Either you are tempted, or have been tempted, or may be tempted, as that man was. The Lord would have Aaron fall, that he might look with compassion upon sinners.

Lastly, it pleased God to let him fall, that he might be a warning to us. *Quomodo tener agnus...* (Alas, how shall the tender lamb stand, when the bellwether of the flock is endangered?) If Aaron, the saint of the Lord (as he is called in this psalm), a man so familiar with God and divine visions, a man who had been so powerful with Moses in working miracles, a man who came so near to God, a man so long conversant with Him, a man who had gone on so many errands of God—as when he went with Moses to Pharaoh—if so holy and great a man as he fell into so great a sin as this, then let us learn to work out our salvation with fear and trembling (Philippians 2:12). "Howl, fir tree; for the cedar is fallen," (Zechariah 11:2). "Be not highminded, but fear," (Romans 11:20). This is the use we are to make of it. So much for the first circumstance.

The second circumstance is: where they made this calf. "In Horeb." There runs all along Arabia a ridge of mountains. It was one mountain, but it had two great tops—Sinai was one, and Horeb the other. You will find them sometimes called by the one name, sometimes by the other. Sometimes the whole mountain is called Sinai, sometimes the whole mountain Horeb, sometimes by the name of the one top, sometimes by the other. Now this is to be observed: they were not yet gone from Horeb. The law had been given in Sinai but a little before, when the Lord charged them out of the fire, "Thou shalt not make unto thee any graven image," (Exodus 20:4). They were still at the foot of the hill, and had not tarried there much more than a month after the law was given. They saw Mount Sinai before them, that higher top, and they could not but remember how Mount Sinai had burned with smoke and fire, and with what earnestness God had charged them, "Thou shalt not make unto thee any graven image, or any likeness," (Exodus 20:4). They were not gone from the mountain—they were still in Horeb. And yet, you see, as it is said in verse 13 of this psalm, "They soon forgat his works; they waited not for his counsel," (Psalm 106:13). So God said to Moses, "Go, get thee down; for thy people, which thou broughtest out of the land of Egypt, have corrupted themselves: They have turned aside quickly out of the way which I commanded them," (Exodus 32:7–8). This shows it clearly. I will not dwell longer on that point.

The third circumstance is: what did they make this calf of? They made it of their golden earrings. "Break off the golden earrings, which are in the ears of your wives, of your sons, and of your daughters, and bring them unto me," (Exodus 32:2). No doubt the servant of God, Aaron, hoped by this to divert them from making the calf. He hoped to turn them from it if he could. He knew that all those people in the eastern lands were much delighted with ornaments, with earrings. They say that even to this day they wear them commonly. And suppose he could persuade the men to part with theirs, yet he thought it impossible to get the women to part with theirs. What? For a woman to part with her jewels and ornaments? This seemed impossible. You know how eager they are for them, that many will even pinch their bellies so they may have something more to put upon their backs. We know that many would rather their bellies go empty than their backs go without adornment. You see how hard it is to persuade women to give up even a trinket or a bag of vanity they carry about with them—but to leave their jewels, their ornaments? He never thought they would do it, though the men might part with theirs. Yet they all did—both men and women.

From this we may observe how easily men and women will part with anything to maintain idolatry.

I cannot tell whether it is (as that father imagined) the pride of our hearts, that we are in love with the works of our own hands, with the devices of our own brains, with the inventions of our own spirits, and therefore we like them because they are our own. Or whether it is the watchfulness of the devil, that roaring lion who goes about seeking whom he may devour (1 Peter 5:8). Or whatever else the cause may be, I do not know. But this I do know: men are *more willing* to part with anything for an idol, for a superstitious worship, than for the *true worship and service of God.*

For this reason, *idolatry* is rightly compared to *whoredom.* You see, a whoremonger will be stingy and sparing enough to his wife and children at home, but he does not care how expensive, how excessive, how lavish he is upon his harlots abroad. So it is in spiritual whoredom: men are never so sparing as in the worship of God, but they are willing to part with anything for the maintaining of idolatry. This eagerness of the people—even to pull their very earrings out of their ears to bestow upon an idol—will rise up to condemn us, who are not willing to pull anything out of our purses for the worship and service of God.

Many men, in this liberal age we live in, are content, with the wise men, to take a long journey to see Christ. Perhaps they are even content to fall down and worship Him. But they are not willing, with those wise men, to open their treasures. Speak to them of opening their treasures, whether for works of piety to God or of charity to men, and then they hesitate, as Naaman the Syrian once said, "In this thing the LORD pardon thy servant," (2 Kings 5:18). Brethren, I could speak much more to this purpose, but I am loath to weary you.

Besides, I know how unnecessary it is in this place. Many times here—twice especially—I have had abundant experience of your forwardness. I have seen how your hearts have been enlarged in bounty toward the enlarging of this place, toward the maintenance of the ministry and the worship of God here. I need not speak of that now.

But I will exhort you now to a work of charity. Do you remember the brief that was read just now, for that poor town of Cambridge? I thought your hearts yearned within you with pity and compassion to hear of almost three thousand poor distressed souls brought into extreme misery through the hand of God in the great plague at Cambridge in August 1630. Brethren, I need say no more. I beseech you, give us, that are your servants in the work of the ministry, leave to come to your houses. "If there be therefore any consolation in Christ, if any comfort of love, if any fellowship of the Spirit, if any bowels and mercies," (Philippians 2:1), then fulfill our joy in this. I beg you, bestow such a blessing upon that poor town and its poor inhabitants, that they may be moved, and we for them, to bless you again, and to pray that God may restore what you give, in the riches of grace here, and of glory hereafter.

Sermon 2

Psalm 106:19–20, "They made a calf in Horeb, and worshipped the molten image, etc."

I began to handle these words the last Lord's day. There are three things in them.

First, the idol: a calf, or young ox, or bullock. Secondly, their sin in this calf, in three things:
First, in making it.
Then, in worshipping it.
And then, in changing their glory into the likeness of it.
"They made a calf in Horeb."
"They worshipped the molten image."
"They changed their glory," *etc.*

The third thing is the root of this sin, the cause of it, where it grew. It grew from forgetfulness of God and His works.

The God they forgot was their Savior.

The works they forgot were,

- First, great works.
- Secondly, wonderful works.
- Thirdly, terrible works.

"They forgat God their Saviour, which had done great things in Egypt; Wondrous works in the land of Ham, and terrible things by the Red sea," (Psalm 106:21–22).

Of the idol I have spoken, and of their first work in making it, in which I considered three circumstances:
First, who made it.
Secondly, where they made it.
Thirdly, of what they made it.

I now go on to the second thing: "They worshipped the molten image."

This was the end for which they wanted it made, and so, consequently, they turned the glory of God into this likeness. Here was their sin. The greater fault was not so much in *making* it—they might have made it without sin—but to make it for this end, to worship it, this was abominable.

Now, because these are dangerous days in which we live, and there is a generation of men that will compass sea and land to make a proselyte, out of my desire to establish your hearts in the true and sincere worship of God, I shall—besides my usual custom—fall upon a matter of controversy and discuss the question between the Church of Rome and us about the worshipping of images. There is a great dispute between them and us about this people's idolatry in worshipping this calf. We believe the sin was exceedingly sinful. Yet they would make it out to be somewhat worse than it was, because they would not be thought to be idolaters, as these were.

The matter will require more time to discuss than I have today. I shall but make an entrance into it. I will tell you what order I will take in handling it.

First, I will show you that the making of an image is not simply forbidden, except it be in way of religion, *to worship and serve God by it, to have high thoughts of God in it*. That is the first. "They made it, and they worshipped it."

Secondly, I will show that all application of divine honor to any image whatsoever is idolatry.

Thirdly, I will show that all idolaters change their God; they change their glory into the likeness of that which they worship.

Fourthly, I will show that the Church of Rome commits as grievous idolatry in worshipping their images as this people did in worshipping the calf.

Lastly, I will show what use we are to make of the whole. I cannot do all today. I shall only begin it, but have patience until I can finish it. And if, in handling these matters, I cite either fathers, or Councils, or traditions of the Church, or history more than I usually do, or more than I think fitting in popular sermons, I pray bear with me and consider whom I deal with—unreasonable men, who will not be satisfied with the sole authority of Holy Scripture.

For the first point: the *making* of an image is no act of idolatry, except it be *by way of religion*, to worship God by it. That is my first proposition. God never, in Scripture, simply forbids the making of an image. He says in the second commandment: "Thou shalt not make unto thee any graven image," (Exodus 20:4). It is true. But you must know that this is a commandment of the first table. Now the first table concerns the *worship* of God. So, you must understand it in relation to the worship of God: "Thou shalt not make an image."

If you will hear God expounding His own law, that it is thus, look in Leviticus 26:1: "Ye shall make you no idols nor graven image, neither rear you up a standing image, neither shall ye set up any image of stone in your land, to bow down unto it: for I am the LORD your God," (Leviticus 26:1). So, it is not the *making* of the image that is forbidden, but bowing down to the image that we have made—or the making it to that end, to bow down. *That* is *idolatry*.

If the making of an image were simply and absolute evil, then surely the same art, skill, and craftsmanship that some men have in carving and engraving of images should never be attributed to the Spirit of God as the author of it. But you shall find that God says: "And I have filled him with the spirit of God, in wisdom, and in understanding, and in knowledge, and in all manner of workmanship, To devise cunning works, to work in gold, and in silver, and in brass, And in cutting of stones, to set them, and in carving of timber, to work in all manner of workmanship," (Exodus 31:3–5). This was said of Bezaleel and Aholiab, to whom God gave wisdom and understanding to do such work, which included images, as you will hear shortly.

God allows the making of images for four uses, which I shall name to you.

First, He allows us to make an image for the distinction of coins. The first coins that I can find mentioned in all of Scripture were stamped with a lamb upon them, and were called for that reason "lambs." You read in Genesis 33:19 that Jacob purchased a field, a parcel of ground, from Hamor the son of Shechem, and he purchased it "for an hundred pieces of money." So it is called there. But the Hebrew phrase is "with an hundred lambs." He bought it with money, as Stephen also says (Acts 7:16). But why does the text say, "with an hundred lambs"? Because it was money stamped with a lamb. So, in Job 42:11, every one of Job's friends brought to him a piece of money. Our translation reads it so, but the Hebrew phrase is "a lamb"—a piece of money so stamped. As we call a piece of gold stamped with an angel an "angel," so the Scripture called that piece of money stamped with a lamb a "lamb." This was the ancient coin I find.

Then that shekel that we often read of in Scripture had two figures upon it: the likeness of the pot of manna on one side, and the likeness of Aaron's rod on the other. Our Lord said to the Herodians, "Shew me a penny. Whose image and superscription hath it? They answered and said, Caesar's" (Luke 20:24). Our Lord did not object to Caesar's image upon a penny, but said, "Render therefore unto Caesar the things which be Caesar's, and unto God the things which be God's," (Luke 20:25). God allows us images for the distinction of coins. That is one.

Secondly, God allows images for ornament. Solomon made a throne of ivory that had six steps to it, and on both sides of the steps, on the right hand and on the left, were lions. There were twelve lions. This was for ornament, an ornament of glory. "There was not the like made in any kingdom," (2 Chronicles 9:19). More than this: the people made a likeness of an ox that eats grass. Solomon made twelve such likenesses of oxen. Look in 2 Chronicles 4:3–4, and you will find that the molten sea stood on twelve oxen that Solomon had made. The people made the likeness of an ox that eats grass; Solomon made twelve likenesses of oxen that eat grass. Solomon was never reproved for this. The people were plagued for theirs. The difference is this: they made it for worship, Solomon made it for ornament. God allows us images for ornament.

And as for the cherubim, you read of so often in Scripture, made in the temple, of what shape they were is hard to say. Josephus says it cannot be affirmed or conjectured. We usually think the face of a cherub was like the face of a man. But you will find there is a difference between them. In Ezekiel 10:14 every beast had four faces: one face was the face of a cherub, another the face of a man, the third the face of a lion, and the fourth the face of an eagle. These were all different faces. So, the face of a cherub and the face of a man are different. But of whatever shape they were, God commanded cherubim to be made in His tabernacle. And Solomon made cherubim—not only those two in the

Most Holy Place, but cherubim all along the walls of the temple, and all upon the veils of the temple, and upon the rims of the vessels, and upon many utensils in the house and service of God. Solomon made cherubim.

Together with them, he made images of lions, bulls, flowers, palm trees, and pomegranates. All these were for ornament.

I conclude then: it is lawful to adorn and beautify our houses. Yes, it is lawful to adorn and beautify the house of God, its walls and windows, with such images as,

First, may not hinder the people in their devotion.

Secondly, are in no danger of being abused to idolatry or superstition. That is my second.

Thirdly, it is lawful to make images for monuments. You know how the brazen serpent was made at God's command in the wilderness. And though it was the likeness of a serpent, yet this was preserved afterward as a monument for the space of seven hundred years, no fewer. For as long as it was a monument, it was preserved. But when it came to be *abused* to idolatry, as you will hear later, then it was broken in pieces. Those statues, those images of our kings, queens, nobles, and great personages in Westminster or St. Paul's, that are set upon their tombs—what end do they serve but to be monuments? A father may set up a monument, a statue, upon the grave of his deceased child; or the child upon the grave of his father. God has allowed this. Christian religion never forbade it. The Christian church has always practiced it—for monuments.

Fourthly, it is lawful to have an image for history. There is a historical use of images. The natural history of beasts, birds, and plants may be set down by imagery. They cannot well be made known without figures of these beasts and birds. How profitable the figures of plants and herbs are in herbals, I think no one questions, who knows the use of herbal or natural histories.

Then secondly, the ecclesiastical histories of the church: the martyrdoms of the saints, the sacred histories of the Bible—the history of Adam and Eve seduced by the serpent, the history of Abel slain by Cain, the history of Abraham sacrificing Isaac, of David killing Goliath, of Solomon judging and giving the child to the right mother; yes, and the history of the passion of Christ. The history of it, I say. This has been approved in the church of God. We read, in Gregory of Nyssa, of the history of the passion of Christ. The historical use of images we do not condemn. Neither God nor the church has ever disallowed it.

So then, to sum it up: God allows us to make an image for the distinction of coins; He allows it for ornament; He allows it for monuments; and He allows the historical use of images in natural history, in sacred history, and in ecclesiastical history.

But let me give some cautions and provisos about these images.

First, no image is *to be made of the Trinity*, for *any* use whatsoever, even if not for religious use. God forbids this in Deuteronomy 4: "Ye heard the voice of the words, but saw no similitude; only ye heard a voice," (Deuteronomy 4:12). Therefore you shall make *no* likeness of Him. So in Isaiah 40:18: "To whom then will ye liken God? or what likeness will ye compare unto him?" To make a visible image of the invisible God is no less unlawful than impossible. To make an image of the Trinity, says Damascene (who, though he was himself a defender of images, yet abhorred this), is folly as well as impiety.

Yet, in spite of this, you will find some such images in the books of Papists. In some of their service books you will see the Trinity pictured with three faces. In others you will see God the Father as an old man, and Christ His Son between His legs, and the dove between them both. These are abominable—such as Christian eyes should not look upon without horror and detestation. No image of the Trinity is ever to be made.

Secondly, no false image, no false representation. I could name many in Popery. To paint the Virgin Mary now in glory in heaven with Christ as a little babe in her arms is a false, lying, blasphemous representation, in no way matching the persons and their true condition. The same may be said of Saint Dunstan and the devil, and of Garnet's face in the straw, publicly shown at Madrid in Spain. Such false representations God condemns, and we abhor.

Thirdly, beware of wanton, lascivious, obscene pictures. These are to be abhorred also. If evil words corrupt good manners, surely lewd and filthy pictures will do it more. Those provocations to lust that enter the heart through the eye stir it much more to uncleanness than those that come in through the ear. He that would guard his heart must guard his eyes.

Fourthly, beware of excessive delight in pictures. There are many among us who have spent even their estates in doting over these rarities and exquisite works. These rules observed, it is lawful for us to make an image—not in the way of religion, not to worship God by it.

Enough of that first point; let me come to a second. I will only touch it. The second is this:

All religious worship, given or bestowed on an image, is *idolatry*.

The application of divine, religious worship to an image is *idolatry*.

First, brethren, know the difference between images and idols; for here they charge us. When we tell them of the second commandment, "Thou shalt not make unto thee any graven image," (Exodus 20:4), they say, you do us wrong to call it so. They argue it should be translated, "Thou shalt not make a graven idol." There is, they say, a great difference between an image and an idol. There is indeed a difference in ecclesiastical usage of speech (and custom must prevail in that kind). Know then how this difference stands. *Imago* in Latin (image), and *eidolon* in Greek (idol), are the same originally. But we must speak in the language of the people. I say, ecclesiastical custom of speech makes a difference between an idol and an image. And what is that difference? I will tell you. Every representation of any creature in heaven above, or in the earth beneath, or in the waters under the earth—that is an image. But if this is applied to the use of religion, then it is an idol, or else it is not. *Omnis consecratio idololatria est* (Every consecration is idolatry), says Tertullian. The consecration of an image makes it an idol. An image is an image, and no more. But if it is set up by way of religion, to serve God by it, then it is an idol.

Let me give you an example I showed even now. The brazen serpent was set up at first at God's appointment. Then miracles were done by the sight of it. As many as were bitten and looked upon it were healed (Numbers 21:9). Then the brazen serpent was a type of Christ: "And as Moses lifted up the serpent in the wilderness, even so must the Son of man be lifted up," (John 3:14). And it was preserved, as you heard before, for seven hundred years. As long as it was a monument, there was no harm in it. But once the people began to burn incense to it—which belonged to the worship and service of God—then Hezekiah, that good king, out of zeal for God's glory, could not endure it any longer, but broke it in pieces. Though it had been set up by God's appointment, though miracles had been done by it, though it was a type of Christ, though it had been preserved seven hundred years, yet he would not spare it. He broke it in pieces and called it *Nehushtan*—"a piece of brass" (2 Kings 18:4). It was nothing more, once divine religious worship was given to it.

Divine religious worship is twofold: Inward and Outward.

Divine inward religious worship is the worship of the *heart and affections*. God requires the whole heart. "My son, give me thine heart," (Proverbs 23:26). He requires *all* the affections of the heart—our love, our fear, our joy, our confidence, our obedience, and subjection. Now, whatever thing it is that draws these affections away from God to itself, that is an idol. That is inward worship.

For this cause (not to give you other examples) the Apostle calls a covetous man an idolater. "But fornication, and all uncleanness, or covetousness, let it not be once named among you, as becometh saints...For this ye know, that no whoremonger, nor unclean person, nor covetous man, who is an idolater, hath any inheritance in the kingdom of Christ and of God", (Ephesians 5:3, 5). He calls covetousness idolatry: "Mortify therefore your members which are upon the earth...covetousness, which is idolatry," (Colossians 3:5). Why is the covetous man an idolater? Because gold and silver withdraw the heart and affections from God.

Look at his affections. What is his love? He loves more the picture of his prince upon his coin than the image of God in his brother. What is his fear? He fears more the loss of his estate than he fears hell. He fears more, to be damaged than to be damned. What is his joy? He rejoices more at the assurance of his money than he rejoices in the assurance of God's favor to him in Christ. What is his confidence? If danger arises, where does he flee? To God? No. "The rich man's wealth is his strong city," (Proverbs 10:15). He flees to his riches. He hopes they will bear him out. He trusts more in uncertain riches than in the living God. "If I have made gold my hope, or have said to the fine gold, Thou art my confidence," (Job 31:24). That is the covetous man.

Then look to his obedience, and you shall see all bends that way. God bids him give; Mammon bids him take, and he takes. God bids him scatter and disperse abroad, and give to the poor; Mammon bids him gather, and he gathers. God bids him relieve; Mammon bids him extort, and he extorts. God bids him lend freely, looking for nothing again; Mammon bids him let his money out at interest, and he does it. See now—Mammon is the god. Mammon has withdrawn the heart and affections, and withdrawn the obedience from God to itself. That which the psalmist says of the heathen, "Their idols are silver and gold, the work of men's hands," (Psalm 115:4), turn but the words, and you may say of covetous men, their silver and gold are their idols. He is an idolater. This is inward worship.

To outward worship belong prayer and thanksgiving, vows and oaths, the building of churches and chapels, the bowing of the body, *all outward observances*, the dedication of ourselves or anything we have to the honor of that which we worship. This is outward worship. Whatever is honored with any part of this religious worship—that is made an idol.

I shall show, when I come to that point, that the Papists, in all these things, bestow God's glory upon an image.

Now, religious worship belongs to God, and to God alone. *Ipsius est et nullius alterius* (It is His, and no other's). God will not allow any part of it to be given to any creature in heaven or earth. If we do, it is idolatry.

What say you to the sun, moon, and stars—glorious creatures? May we not worship them?

No. They are glorious creatures indeed, but they are such as God has made to serve us; He did not make us to serve them.

But what say you to angels? We are somewhat lower than angels; may we not worship them?

Mark what the angel said to John in Revelation 19:10: "And I fell at his feet to worship him. And he said unto me, See thou do it not: I am thy fellowservant, and of thy brethren that have the testimony of Jesus: worship God." We are not servants to them. They and we are fellow servants to one and the same God. "See thou do it not: worship God."

O, but what say you to the Virgin Mary? Is it not lawful to worship her?

I will answer in the words of the old church: *Mariam nemo colat*—let no man worship the Virgin Mary.

Let the Virgin Mary be honored, say they, and let her be called blessed in all generations; but let God the Father, Son, and Holy Ghost be worshipped. Let no man worship the Virgin Mary.

No, I go further still. The very human nature of Christ, the manhood of Christ, is not to be worshipped any otherwise than as it is united to the person of the Son of God. I will tell you the confession of the primitive Fathers: *Confitemur Dominum nostrum Jesum Christum in carne adorandum, sed non secundum carnem.* We confess that our Lord Jesus Christ is to be worshipped in the flesh, in the manhood, but not *according* to the manhood.

Nestorius, that blasphemous heretic, divided the person of Christ. We believe there is but one person—God and man. He made two persons in Christ. He made one the Son of God, who was not the son of Mary; and another the son of Mary, who was not the Son of God. And yet he believed that the son of Mary, who was not the Son of God, was to be adored. The fathers in the church of God abhorred this and condemned the doctrine of Nestorius for idolatry: *Damnamus idololatriam Nestorii*—we condemn the idolatry of Nestorius.

Mark this, I pray. If the very manhood of Christ may not be adored and worshipped with religious worship, except as it is united to the person of the Son of God—if the manhood of Christ, when worshipped apart, is an idol (for the word idolatry implies so much)—if it be an idol, not being united to the person of the Son of God, then surely the images of Christ must necessarily *be idols*, since they are in *no way united* either to the Godhead of Christ or yet to His manhood.

I should have said more of this point if I had had time. I shall go on, by God's grace, the next Sabbath.

Sermon 3

Psalm 106:19–20, "They made a calf in Horeb, and worshipped the molten image, *etc.*"

Out of my desire to establish your hearts in the true and sincere worship of God, I thought it good to discuss the question between the Church of Rome and us about the worshipping of images. This order I have proposed to myself:

First, to show that the making of all kinds of images is not forbidden.

Secondly, that the worshipping of images is idolatry.

Thirdly, that the idolater, in worshipping an image, turns his glory into the likeness of that image.

Fourthly, that the worshipping of images, as it is taught and practiced in the Church of Rome, is outright idolatry.

Fifthly, I promised to show you the use of all these.

The first two points I have handled. Now I come to my third proposition, and it is this: the idolater, in worshipping an image, changes his glory into that image.

Mark the words of the text: "They worshipped the molten image; and in doing that, they changed their glory." But I must tell you, I find the words read two ways: sometimes, *his glory*, and sometimes, *their glory*. "They changed their glory." The Greek Septuagint reads it the first way, *his glory*. If you take it so—*his glory*, that is, the glory of God—then we must distinguish the glory of God. The glory of God is twofold:

- There is the absolute glory of God.
- There is the relative glory of God.

The absolute glory of God is that incomprehensible, ineffable majesty of the Deity, dwelling in light that no man can approach. This glory it pleased God, in some measure, to communicate to the creatures, to angels, and to men, in such a way as is convenient and possible for them to partake. This is the absolute glory of God; this cannot be changed, no more than God himself can.

But there is also a relative glory of God—that glory which men give to God in worshipping him. That glory may be changed. And indeed the Gentiles changed it, as the Apostle says: "They changed the glory of the uncorruptible God into an image made like to corruptible man," (Romans 1:23). And in this way the Israelites here changed his glory. If you read the words as the Septuagint does, "They changed his glory." But I do not like that reading; the other is better. "They changed their glory"—their own glory. What was that? By their glory is meant God himself. "They changed their glory," that is, they changed their God. Scripture will make this plain. "Hath a nation changed their gods, which are yet no gods? but my people have changed their glory for that which doth not profit," (Jeremiah 2:11).

Let me observe something from the very words. God may be called the glory of his people in two ways:

1. As he is the author of their glory.
2. As he is the matter of their glory.

In this way old Simeon, when he had Christ in his arms, called him "the glory of thy people Israel," (Luke 2:32). "But thou, O LORD, art a shield for me; my glory, and the lifter up of mine head," (Psalm 3:3). Among the many privileges that belonged to the people of the Jews, the Apostle names one, and that was this: "To whom pertaineth...the glory," (Romans 9:4). What glory was that?

We may take it, as some do, for the glory of the covenant—God was their glory by covenant. Or else you may take it for the glory of miracles, by which God brought them out of the land of Egypt. Or else you may take it for the glory of divine vision and revelation that God granted to them.

Or (which I take especially), by "glory" you may mean the ark, which was the sign of God's presence. And therefore, Phinehas's daughter-in-law, when she heard that the ark of God was taken, said, "The glory is departed from Israel"; and she named her son, born at that time, Ichabod—"Where is glory?" For she said again, "The glory is departed from Israel: for the ark of God is taken," (1 Samuel 4:21–22).

We may speak what we will of other glories, but the true glory of any nation is this: to *have* God for their God. The gracious and glorious presence of God, in all his holy and blessed ordinances, according to his word—that is the glory of any nation under heaven.

It is our happiness that we have this glory yet among us. The prophet Ezekiel, in chapters 9–11, shows how the glory of God departed from Jerusalem. It did not depart all at once, but by degrees it went away.

First, the glory of the Lord removed from between the cherubim, where it was, and came to the threshold of the house. There it stayed a while, as if to see if the people would turn to him by repentance. Then it removed to the east gate of the Lord's house, the farthest gate, and stayed there a while. Then it moved to the midst of the city. And from the midst of the city, it went to the mountain on the east side—the Mount of Olives—completely out of the city.

We have the glory of God yet in our land. May it be the good pleasure of God to continue this glory among us until Jesus Christ comes in glory with all his saints. But, brethren, does not this glory of God seem to withdraw? Does it not seem to move away? O, should God withdraw his word from us and the profession of it—should God remove the candlestick out of his place, should God withdraw his gracious presence in all his ordinances—then I tell you, mothers, what you should name your children that are born next: Ichabod, "Where is glory?" when God is gone from you.

I have read of foolish nations that were accustomed to *chain* their gods, to keep them from departing. Surely, our God cannot be chained or fettered. Yet there is a way to hold him still, when he seems to be departing. "I held him, and would not let him go," (Song of Solomon 3:4). "I will not let thee go, except thou bless me," (Genesis 32:26). When our blessed Lord seemed to the two men going to Emmaus as if he would leave them, the Scripture says, "They constrained him, saying, Abide with us," (Luke 24:29). We may constrain our God. There is a holy violence we may use with our God, by repentant tears and importunate prayers, by which we may keep him with us still. Tertullian calls it a holy violence, pleasing and acceptable to God.

But I will not dwell longer on the words. Now I come to the thing itself.

"They changed their glory"—that is, they *changed* their God. How may a people *change* their God? They may change their God two ways:

1. When they forsake him and set up and worship some other god in his stead, as the people forsook the Lord and served Baal and Ashtaroth (Judges 2:13). This is the grossest kind of idolatry. This is a breach of the first commandment.
2. Or secondly, a people may change their God, when they change the truth of God into a lie, when they represent and worship God in an Image, when they represent God in a corporeal, a visible, a finite, a circumscribed Majesty; this is to change a God: this is against the second Commandment. And you must know, that in this way the people changed their God here at

this time; for, we do not think that they made this calf to be their god. Their sin was bad enough, let not us make it worse than it was. They had cast off now all religion, and the fear of God, let us not think they had cast off sense and reason with it. Can we imagine that this people were such calves, as to think that the calf that they themselves had made yesterday was the very God that brought them out of Egypt three months before the calf was made? Never imagine that; they did not take this calf to be their god. What then? They took it to be a *figurative sign* of their God. I know they call it their god; "These be thy gods, O Israel, which brought thee up out of the land of Egypt," (Exodus 32:4). Or, as it is in Nehemiah, "This is thy God that brought thee up out of Egypt," (Nehemiah 9:18). But, as this image is called a calf in my text, "They made a calf in Horeb," though it was no calf, but the image of a calf: so they called it their god; but they did not think it to be their god. They took it as an image of their God, as a figurative sign of their God: therefore Aaron proclaims, "Tomorrow is a feast to the LORD," (Exodus 32:5); not to the calf, but to Jehovah, whom they worshipped in the calf.

I pray mark this rule that I shall give you: The truth of God is turned into a lie, and God is changed to the image that is worshipped; though God himself, and none but he, be worshipped in that image, I say, God is changed into that image that is worshipped for him, though the true God, and none but he, be worshipped in that image.

Here is its reason: the rule of *divine worship* is not the will of the worshipper, but it is the will of Him that is worshipped. Now, it was never God's will to be worshipped in an image. Take a similitude: suppose a subject, a vassal, should devise an honor of his own brain to his sovereign, to his king; and he should set up a toad, and he will have it in a glass, and come every morning and bow to that toad; and being asked why he did so, he should say, O, I do it not to the toad, but to the honor of my sovereign and prince: do you think this prince will like well to be resembled by a toad?

I tell you, brethren, there is a thousand times a greater disproportion between Almighty God and an image set up for him, than there is between a prince and a toad. Not to speak of that infinite inequality and distance that is between God and a mortal man; there is a great distance even between a toad and an idol, a great difference. *For,*

The toad is the workmanship of God; an idol, as it is an idol, is the workmanship of man. A toad is a living creature; it has sense and motion. The image is a senseless block; it has neither life nor motion. Therefore, hear how it pleases the Spirit of God in Scripture to call consecrated images. He calls them sometimes lies, sometimes vanities, sometimes (yes, often) abominations, sometimes dunghill gods, sometimes devils. "They...worshipped devils, and idols of gold, and silver, and brass, and stone, and of wood: which neither can see, nor hear, nor walk," (Revelation 9:20). Hear how the Spirit of God in Scripture shows his detestation of all images in his service. Listen to how he thunders in the second commandment: "Thou shalt not make unto thee any graven image...thou shalt not bow down thyself to them, nor serve them," (Exodus 20:4–5). Hear what the prophet Isaiah says: "They shall be turned back, they shall be greatly ashamed, that trust in graven images, that say to the molten images, Ye are our gods," (Isaiah 42:17). Hear what the Apostle says in the New Testament: "Little children, keep yourselves from idols. Amen," (1 John 5:21).

I pray, look over the Bible, and see if you ever find any of God's children (except at such times as they had corrupted their ways) worshipping images. Enough out of Scripture against images.

Now, because we are in this controversy dealing with such men whom the authority of Scripture does not satisfy, such unreasonable men as are *not content* with the authority of Scripture; and because they say this stands upon tradition, the worshipping of images in the church: I pray give me leave a little, besides my custom, to show you the testimony of the fathers, the determination of Councils, and the long tradition of the church against images. Of every one a word, and some few of many. There is no point in which a man may be so copious as in this.

First, for Fathers: *Fieri non potest, ut simulacrum colens Deum noverit* (It is not possible that a man should know God and yet be a suppliant to an image), so says Origen. *Nulla est religio, ubi simulachrum colitur* (There is no religion where there is a worshipping of images), says Lactantius. *Indignum est, ut imago hominis mortui ab homine colatur, qui imago est Dei viventis* (It is a most unworthy thing that the image of a dead man should be worshipped by man, who is the image of the living God), says Tertullian. "We make no figure or representation of the saints," says Anthelopius, bishop of Hippo. "We have no need of them," says Ambrose: "God will not be worshipped by a stone." "We worship no image," says Augustine, "but that image which is the same that God himself is"—he means Christ, the substantial image of the Father. I could go on, but this is enough.

Come then to Councils. The Council of Elvira in Spain—at that time, through the negligence of bishops, images had crept into the church—decreed there should be no pictures in the church.[4] The Council of Constantinople condemned all images in the church of God. And so did the Council of Frankfort under Charles the Great.

For the tradition of the church: For three hundred years after Christ, it is confessed by some of our adversaries themselves, there were no images in the

[4] The 36th canon of the Synod of Elvira (in Spain between 300 and 303) prohibited images as a hindrance to the spiritual worship of God.

churches of God. Three hundred years after that—six hundred years after Christ—then began images in the churches; then the people began to yield *some* worship to them. Gregory the Great, bishop of Rome, condemned the worshipping of them. He allowed them to be in the church, and in that he did ill, for they were provocations to idolatry; yet he condemned the worshipping of them. In this way it continued six hundred years after Christ. Between six and eight hundred years, there arose a great stir in the church of God, between the Eastern and Western churches, about the worshipping of images. The bishops of the West, under Rome, were all for images; the good emperor of the East was against it. There was a bloody war about it, and it continued for above a hundred years. Then Irene the empress, during the minority of her son—a cruel, idolatrous woman (and mark it well: idolatry is always cruel)—caused the second Nicene Council to be called. And there, for the first time, was decreed the worshipping of images in the church of God, in the year of our Lord 788. Until then, images were *never* appointed publicly to be worshipped in the church. Yes, even after that time, the worshipping of images did not gain a quiet and settled profession in the church of God. Charles the Great, emperor in the West, mightily opposed it. He called his bishops together at Frankfort, and they strongly opposed the worshipping of images.

Yes, mark this, brethren, a duty that concerns us in our kingdom. Charles the Great sent the acts of that second idolatrous Nicene Council to our bishops in England, to know how they liked it. They said, "Alas, we find in those acts many things against Christian religion, especially this: that the worshipping of images is decreed, which the church of God curses." Mark that: our bishops, the forefathers of the church in England, about eight hundred years ago, held that to be a doctrine which the church of God curses. And that against all the tables of God's law, against the preaching of the prophets, against the institution of the apostles, against the custom of the old church, against the practice of the primitive church, against the clear testimonies of the Fathers, against the determination of councils, against a continued tradition for almost eight hundred years together. "The beauty of the church" (as one complains) "in defiance of God and man, is now polluted with the filth of paganism; and Christian churches are pestered, as much as ever the heathen temples were, with idols."

I come now to the proof of that—that is the fourth point: that the worshipping of images, as it is taught and practiced in the Church of Rome, is plain paganism and idolatry.

The pagan and the popish idolatry are all one. I say, the worshipping of images, as it is taught and practiced in the Church of Rome, is plain heathenish idolatry.

How is it taught, and how is it practiced? For the doctrine of their church, it is hard for a man to set it down. The determination of the Council of Trent about it is like a nose of wax; you may turn it *any* way. They tell us of our divisions among ourselves; but it is a wonder to see how they interfere and strike one another in the point of worshipping images. It is hard to say what they teach. But I will tell you this much. Isolanius the Jesuit says, "This is the constant opinion of the divines of our church, that images are to be worshipped with the same worship that is due to him whose image it is." This was the doctrine of Thomas Aquinas, whom they count a saint. This was the doctrine of all his followers. This was the doctrine of Nauclantus, a bishop in Italy, upon Romans 1. "We do not," says he, "worship before an image, as some men are wont casually to speak; but we worship the image itself, and that with the same worship that is due to him whose image it is." Peter de Palude, a great professor of divinity in Spain, says, "This doctrine is the only true and pious doctrine, agreeable to the decrees of the Christian faith." He names nineteen of the special schoolmen who were all of this opinion besides himself. We take this, then, to be the doctrine of the Church of Rome: that images are to be worshipped with the same worship that is due to him whose image it is.

They that have traveled into foreign parts have found that the practice of that church is as bad as these theories. It is confessed by some of the more modest among them, that their people have grown to a kind of piety that differs little from impiety. You will say the same if you *consider*,

First, the image itself.

Then, the worship that is given to that image.

Then, come to their rites and ceremonies in yielding these acts. I pray read at your leisure the sixth chapter of Baruch; you will say it is an Apocryphal book, and I confess it is so. But with them it is Canonical, and so it is good Scripture against them. The author of that chapter shows what the people shall see when they come to Babylon; he said, there you shall see an image of gold, or of silver, or of wood, or brass, or stone: you shall see it clad in purple, with a scepter in its hand; or perhaps trimmed up garishly. You shall see such an image carried upon men's shoulders in a solemn procession, and a number of people before and behind it, adoring and worshipping it. You shall see the priests with their shaven heads and beards taking off those offerings that are offered to those images, and bestowing them upon common harlots. You shall see, he said, candles lighted to them, you shall see perfume burned to them, you shall hear vows made to them, you shall see oblations and offerings given to them: and all this to such an image as is no better, he said, than a scarecrow in a garden of cucumbers.

Now those that have ever seen the processions that are in Paris, or the Lady of Heige at Iquiers in Flanders, or have ever seen the worship in Italy or Spain;

they can bear witness that they have seen all these things done, and a number of fooleries more besides these.

We may think they have somewhat to say for themselves; and in a word or two, you shall hear it.

First, they say, they do not worship the image, but they worship him *in* that image whose image it is.

Mark, first, they have no excuse for the worshipping of images, but the same that the heathens had. Their worship is heathenish, and so is their excuse. For when the Fathers, in the first years of the Church, challenged the heathen for the worshipping of images: What, they said, do you think us such blocks, as to worship these blocks? They have the same.

Again, it is not true that they say; for, as I said before, they conclude they worship the image. Bellarmine proves that the worship properly *belongs* to the image.

Again, suppose they intended not to worship the image, but God in it: Know that the rule of divine worship is not man's intention, but God's will. Mark it in the example I gave before, of a man honoring his prince in a toad. We inquire not of the will of the worshipper, but of him that is worshipped. Let them show that it is God's will to be worshipped in an image, and we will not charge them with idolatry.

But, they say, do we not do reverence to the chair of state, in honor to the king, when the king is not there?

We do, indeed a civil reverence to it; but who appointed an image to be the chair of state to the King of heaven? The reverence we do to the chair of state is according to the will of the prince; it is his will it should be done. But where can they tell us it is the will of God that we should reverence and worship him in a base inglorious abomination?

Yes, but they say, images in the Church of God have been accounted laymen's books.

It is true, they have called them so; but I say that again, they are books prohibited. They are not books that come forth *cum privilegio*. God does not allow such books as these. When the bishops in their churches were faithful in their places, and taught the people out of the Word, the people did not need these books. But when teachers came to be idols, then idols came to be teachers.

Yes, but they say, the worship that we give to images, we give it not properly; it is improperly, it is by analogy, representatively, reductively—these are Bellarmine's words, and many more such distinctions.

O brethren, these are the men that know how to rob God of his glory, and yet they know how to deceive and delude the world with distinctions. There is no place so plain but they can elude it with distinctions. But in the meantime, what wrong is it to God's people to bring them to horrible gross idolatry, and then to seek to work and wind them out with such new distinctions, as the poor people do not understand, nor perhaps they themselves?

If any man desire to be better satisfied about the point of worshipping of images, I desire him to read the third Homily in our Church, set forth by the Church against the peril of *Idolatry*, and he shall find abundant satisfaction.

There is yet one point to be handled: it is the use that we are to make of this, and of the whole history. But the time is past, I must leave it for the next day.

Sermon 4

Psalm 106:19-22, "They made a calf in Horeb, and worshipped the molten image. Thus they changed their glory into the similitude of an ox that eateth grass. They forgat God their saviour, which had done great things in Egypt; Wondrous works in the land of Ham, and terrible things by the Red sea."

There remains now but one thing more concerning this worshipping of images, and that is the use you are to make of all this that you have heard concerning it. It is this, by way of exhortation: Let me exhort you to *hate, abhor, and detest* all idolatry if it be image-worship, whether heathenish or popish.

Holy David, in Psalm 119, brings many arguments to prove his love to God and to his Word; and one argument above all others (for he repeats it often) is this—his *hatred of false ways.* He means false doctrine, all falsehood in doctrine, and falsehood in life. In verse 113, "I hate all inventions; but thy law do I love." Verse 163, "I hate and abhor all falsehood, but thy law do I love." And in this way, he goes on in many places more. Now then, if our hatred of falsehood is an argument of our love to the truth; if such as is our hatred to error, is our love to true religion; then surely, brethren, we are fallen from our first love, because we are fallen from our first hatred of Popery and superstition. We are grown now to have a better opinion of image-worship than we had before. We are grown almost to a very neutrality in religion.

The desire of my soul is to preserve your hearts upright in the holy, sincere worship of God: therefore, I pray, let me commend four caveats to you, with which I will conclude this point.

The first is this, it is that of Saint John, 1 John 5:21, "Babes, keep yourselves from idols." Mark, he says not from idolatry, but from idols; not from the service of idols, but from idols themselves, from such images as may be abused to idolatry.

God in the old law forbade his people to desire the gold of an image: they may not desire so much as the gold of an image. "For it will be as a snare to thee," said God, Deut. 7:25. David met with the Philistines' images; it is likely they were of gold, or silver, or the like: and what did he with them? He burned them every one, 2 Sam. 5:21.

The brazen serpent, though it was set up at the first (as you heard) by God's own command; though there were miracles wrought by the sight of it; though it was kept seven hundred years, as an excellent monument of God's mercy; though it was a type and figure of Christ, "Even as the brazen serpent was lifted up in the wilderness, so shall the Son of man be lifted up:" yet good Hezekiah, when he saw incense burned to it, would not spare it, but he took the serpent, and broke it, and stamped it in pieces, and called it Nehushtan—it was a piece of brass, and no more.

What did Moses in this history, when he saw the calf? Though it was made of gold, and there might have been some use of gold among the poor people, it might have done good to a number of them; yet he would not keep the gold. He burned it in the fire, he stamped it to powder, he beat it as small as dust, Deut. 9:21. And he was not yet revenged enough of this image; he cast the dust into the brook that ran out of Horeb, and made the people drink of that water. He would not have the least memorial of this image left.

Let me tell you but one more history out of the Church: Epiphanius, that good bishop, came to a church, and found a veil in the church, wherein there was an image of Christ, or of some saint. "For," he said, "I remember not whose it was, but I took it, and tore it, and wrote to John, Bishop of Jerusalem, under whose charge that church was, that he should not suffer such veils in the church, against Christian religion."

These are good patterns for magistrates in church or commonwealth; but these are no precedents for private men in public places, out of a pretense of zeal, in a tumultuous manner, to attempt any such public reformation. Men may do, as Jacob did at home; every man reform his own household, bury his own images, at home. But private men must learn that golden rule of Saint Augustine: to correct what they can within the compass of their own calling, and what they cannot, to mourn for; to mourn and to cry to God, that he would please to send his Son, to take whatsoever offends out of his kingdom. This is the first caveat: take heed of images. To take heed of sin, is to take heed of the occasions of sin.

My second caveat is, take heed of familiar conversation with these image-worshippers. All society with them is not unlawful; there may be a lawful society even with idolaters, in regard of public conversation. But take heed of society with them in regard of inward acquaintance with them; it is dangerous. Let a good man be joined with an evil man, you seldom see the evil bettered by the good; but the good is easily corrupted and spoiled by the evil. A whole lump of dough will not sweeten a little leaven, but a little leaven will sour a whole lump of dough. "If any man that is called a brother be an idolater," said Paul, "with such a man eat not," 1 Cor. 5:11.

The Pharisees in old time were so careful of their carriage among the Gentiles and Samaritans, that they would not so much as eat of a Samaritan's bread, nor drink of a Samaritan's cup, nor warm themselves at a Samaritan's fire. They would not wear a Samaritan's garment, nor read a Samaritan's book. It is said of John the Evangelist, that he refused to wash himself in that bath wherein Cerinthus the heretic had washed. Polycarp could not be gotten to salute Marcion the heretic. Eusebius of Vercelli would not receive meat in prison from the hands of the Arians. You know what Saint John says: "Whosoever says, God speed to them, is partaker with them in their sin," (2 John 10).

It is a childish thing I shall tell you of, but you may perceive by it how children were trained up in the detestation of heresy. Theodoret tells of it: At Samosatum, the children playing with a ball, refused to play with it after the ball by chance had touched Lucius the heretical bishop, or the donkey that he rode on; they cast the ball into the fire, and would play no more with it. We have a story of Thosmos, that being about to be thrown, when he was dead, into the grave of an heretical bishop, a voice was heard in the grave, "Touch me not, heretic." I avouch not this for truth, but I told you what the Apostle said; If any man be called a brother, and be an idolater, with such a one eat not.

Surely, brethren, we are grown a little too familiar with them, we are too bold with these image-mongers; we match with them, we consult with them, we confer with them, we converse with them; perhaps we find such delight in their company, that we cannot be merry unless they be in our company; we cannot eat our meat, unless they carve it; we cannot sleep, unless they rock the cradle: no wonder, brethren, if we are drawn away.

But let me give you a third caveat: Take heed of beholding idol-service out of the curiosity of the eye. Many men will go to mass, or idol-service; they say they mean not to adore, they will not worship, they go but to see. May they not go see it?

I tell you, that sight is very dangerous, that curiosity of the eye is a branch of the concupiscence of the eye, which, if it is not mortified, may be the occasion of many sins. Idolatry is called in Scripture by the name of whoredom. Lust gets into the heart by the eye. It is a hard matter for the body to be kept clean, if the eye is full of adultery. Job made a covenant with his eyes to abridge them of liberty in matters of indifferency.

Let me tell you a story that Saint Augustine has in the sixth book of his *Confessions*, chapter 8. He tells of Alypius his dear friend, who went to Rome to study the law. At Rome there were usually those gladiatorial sports, bloody, sword-killing sports; they killed men in sport. He could not be persuaded by his companions to see those sports; they desired him, but by no means would he go. At last (said Saint Augustine) by a familiar violence they drew him once to go and see those bloody sports. "Well," said he, "I will go, but I will be absent while I am there, I will not look on it." He went, and when he came, he sat there among the rest, but he shut his eyes, and would not see any of those sports, until at length there was a man wounded, and then the people shouted. He had shut his eyes, but he had not stopped his ears; he heard the shout, and would see what was the matter; he looked about, and, seeing the wounded man, he then desired to see a little more. In this way (said Saint Augustine) he grew at the last not to be the same man he was when he came there, but to be as one of the company to which he came; and, after that time, he desired to see it a second, and a third time; and, at last, he came to be, not only a companion of those that went there, but would be a guide to them; he would go, not as one among them, but one of the forwardest. And in this way he continued a while, until it pleased God, by a mighty hand, to deliver him from this vanity.

The eyes are the windows of the body, and if we do not shut them up against allurements, we may soon be forced to cry out, as they did in Jeremiah 9:21, "Death is entered in at the windows." "Lord," said David, "turn away mine eyes, that they behold not vanity." Idols are called vanities often in Scripture. Surely, we should make a covenant with our eyes, that they be not the occasion of our falling. I said it the other day; I conclude with it now: he that would have an eye to his heart, must have a heart to his eye.

My fourth caveat is this: take heed how you allow yourselves to live in any known sin without repentance; for this is the way for which God gives men over to the sin of idolatry. Unrepented errors in life breed errors in judgment. Those, 2 Thessalonians 2:10–11, that will not embrace the love of the truth, that they may be saved (said the Apostle), those men shall have strong delusions to believe lies. I conclude all with what the Apostle, speaking of the heathen, said, Romans 1:25: They knew God. The heathen had some knowledge of God, but they were not careful to glorify him as God, but were unthankful. What punishment came upon them for it? This—their foolish heart grew full of darkness, and when they professed themselves wise men, they became fools. Fools! Why? How did they play the fools?

Said the Apostle (which is the *very* phrase that is here): Because, when they knew God, they did not care to glorify him as God, but were unthankful; therefore God gave them over to this blindness, to turn the glory of the incorruptible God, to the image of corruptible man, and of four-footed beasts, and they served and worshipped the creature more than the Creator, who is God over all, and blessed forever.

In this way, beloved, I have now completed that great point concerning the worshipping of images.

Now I come to the last thing in my text, that is the *root* of this sin, where this sin of theirs sprang: it was from forgetfulness of God, and of his works.

"They forgot God their Saviour," *etc.*

The words are many, and many things may be observed out of them. I will run them first over with a brief paraphrase, and then speak of that sin that was the cause of this idolatry: the forgetfulness of God.

[They forgot God.] There was one of the tribes that was called the tribe of Manasseh; Manasseh had this name, of forgetfulness. When I look over this Psalm, it seems to me this people should all be of that tribe, they were so forgetful. In verse 7, "They remembered not the multitude of his mercies." There the Spirit of God speaks of their forgetfulness. Then, in verse 13, "They soon forgot his works." They made haste, and forgot them, as the words are. And now here again, "They forgot God their Saviour." Three times the Spirit of God in this Scripture speaks of their forgetfulness of God.

It was but three months ago since God brought them out of the land of Egypt: it was little more than one month ago since God appeared to them in a fearful manner upon Mount Sinai, with thunder, and lightning, and earthquakes; and yet see, they have already forgotten God.

[God their Saviour.] Savior: the word is sometimes taken strictly in the Scripture, in a narrow sense; and sometimes it is taken in a larger sense.

If you take the word in the narrow sense, then a Savior is one who saves from sin, from the punishment of sin, from God's wrath, from hell, and from eternal damnation. In this sense our Lord is called a Savior. You know what the angel said to the shepherds: "For unto you is born this day in the city of David a Savior, which is Christ the Lord," (Luke 2:11). And even his very name declares this; Jesus signifies a Savior, and the reason is given by the angel: because "he shall save his people from their sins," (Matthew 1:21). He saves them,

First, from the guilt of sin.

Then he saves them from the punishment of sin.

Then he saves them from the power of sin.

This is the sense of the word Savior when you take it strictly.

But you may take the word more broadly, and then a Savior is one who is a deliverer, a preserver—whether from wrong, from afflictions, from oppressions, from dangers, or from temporal death. A Savior, that is, a Preserver. In this sense the Apostle says, "For therefore we both labour and suffer reproach, because we trust in the living God, who is the Saviour of all men, specially of those that believe," (1 Timothy 4:10). That is, he is the preserver of all men, but especially of believers. In this sense the word is used here: God was their Savior, that is, their Preserver.

And consider this:

First, the evils from which he preserved them—and they were many.

Then, the means by which he preserved them—and they were mighty.

Then, the end for which he preserved them—and that was glorious: that they should be a holy people, a peculiar treasure to himself. Consider, I say, the evils from which, the means by which, and the end for which they were preserved; and then no people could more rightly call God their Saviour than this people could. Yet behold—they forgot God their Saviour.

Yes, and they forgot his works. The works of God are described here in three ways:

- Great works.
- Wonderful works.
- Terrible works.

Great works in Egypt. Wonderful works in the land of Ham (and the land of Ham is the same as Egypt). And terrible works by the Red Sea.

[Great works.] The works of God are either works of nature or works of grace.

The works of nature are either works of creation, or works of providence in preserving what has been created.

The works of grace are many. The chief of them, on which all the rest depend, is the incarnation of the Son of God—that great mystery of godliness, God manifest in the flesh (1 Timothy 3:16). That was the great work of grace.

Then comes the redemption of mankind by his blood. The election of some to salvation before the foundation of the world was laid. The calling of them in God's appointed time. The justification of them through the blood of our crucified Jesus. The sanctification of them by God's Holy Spirit. The resurrection of their bodies, and the glorification of them. All these are works of grace.

Now, all the works of God—whether they are works of nature or of grace—are great works. There is not a work of creation that is not a great work. The ant is a small creature, yet it is a great work. The making of an ant is as great a work as the creation of an elephant. To God it is all one; he can as easily make an elephant as an ant. Indeed, *Deus maximus in minimis* (God is greatest in the least). A man may rightly say that. God shows himself greatest in the least of his creatures. If you observe carefully, you may see how great God is in every small creature.

The smaller the watch that you carry to tell the time of day, the greater the skill of the workman who made it. In the same way, in every small work it becomes evident how great God is. There is no work so little that it is not a great work when rightly considered. The works of creation are great works.

But there are some works greater than others—those in which the divine attributes are most clearly revealed. Works in which the great wisdom of God appears, or his great goodness, or his great power, or his great truth, or his great mercy, or his great justice. The works in which these attributes of divine majesty shine forth most plainly are called great works.

Therefore, the works of redemption are greater than the works of creation; the works of grace are greater than the works of nature.

But this people had seen great works in both kinds—great works of nature and great works of grace.

There were works of nature; let me name just one or two of them. The multiplication of the people in Egypt. When they first came down to Egypt, they were only seventy souls, seventy descendants of Jacob, no more. They were in Egypt for only two hundred and fifteen years, and much of that time under heavy oppression—burdened with labor, beaten with blows, crushed with injuries. Yet see how they multiplied: this vine, bleeding under the knife, bore an abundance of fruit. Like chamomile, the more it was pressed down, the more it spread. In two hundred and fifteen years they grew into a multitude, so that when they came out of Egypt there were numbered six hundred thousand men from twenty years old and upward, besides women and children. This multiplication was a great work of God—a work of nature.

Then consider their preservation there, how wonderfully they were kept, in spite of their enemies and how all their possessions were preserved as well. The land of Goshen was spared from the swarms of flies that filled the rest of Egypt. Their cattle were preserved from the plague that killed the herds throughout Egypt. The land of Goshen had light, while all Egypt was in thick darkness. Their households were spared when the firstborn of all Egypt perished. This preservation was a great work of God.

Another work—perhaps even greater—was their deliverance out of Egypt. Their preservation was great; their bringing out was just as great. They came out, in spite of Pharaoh and his servants. And they came out strong, with vigor in their bodies, with blood flowing in their veins and marrow in their bones. The Scripture says, "There was not one feeble person among their tribes," (Psalm 105:37). Here were great works—but these were works of nature, works of multiplication and preservation.

Now, hear of the great works of grace. The adoption of this people as God's firstborn. The separation of them from all other nations of the earth, to be to God a holy nation, a royal priesthood, his own peculiar treasure. The revealing of his promises, especially that great promise, that from their line would come the blessed seed—the Lord in whom all the nations of the earth would be blessed. The giving of the Law; no nation had it but they. As the psalmist says, "He hath not dealt so with any nation: and as for his judgments, they have not known them," (Psalm 147:20).

Here were great works of nature, and great works of grace. Yet, in the face of all this, the unthankfulness of the people showed itself: they forgot God their Savior, who had done these great things for them in Egypt.

Then came wonderful works too—*mirabilia.* There are four kinds of wondrous things.

First, there are wonders of nature—*mirabilia naturae.* Hidden marvels in creation: that the lodestone should draw iron to itself, yet its power is restrained when a diamond is near it. That a diamond cannot be broken with a hammer on an anvil, but crumbles when smeared with goat's blood. That the flesh of a dead peacock does not rot—Augustine himself claimed to have tested it over a full year. That a fountain in Libya pours water so cold by day that none can drink it, and so hot by night that none can touch it. These, and a thousand more, are wonders of nature—unexplained, but all the work of God.

Second, there are wonders of art—*mirabilia artis.* The ancients spoke of seven wonders of the world. One was in Egypt, the pyramids. Another, above them all, was a marvel of construction, though in truth nothing but a monument of vanity and excess. Its skill came from God, though its purpose was sinful.

Third, there are wonders of Satan—*mirabilia Satanae*. Works of power that Satan and his instruments, the magicians and sorcerers, can perform. The fallen angels were not stripped of their natural power; their ability to do harm is still as great as the power of good angels to do good. The devil can move over the earth in little time. In Job's narrative he raised tempests, sent fire from heaven, and swept away households. He carried the body of our Lord from the wilderness to the pinnacle of the temple, and then to a high mountain. He has spoken through images—the voices in heathen idols were the devil's voice. And if, as the Papists claim, some of their images have spoken too—"You have written well of me, Thomas," said to Aquinas—I do not doubt it was the devil's voice. The devil knows the hidden properties, sympathies, and antipathies of things. He can do many astonishing feats. But though he can do wonders, he cannot do true miracles. His marvels are *mira*, not *miracula*.

Fourth, there are the wonders of God—*mirabilia Dei*. In truth, every work of God is wondrous, but some are above nature and rightly called miracles. These are works beyond the reach of natural power—what only God himself can do. The devil can use natural causes, but he cannot suspend or overrule them. Only God works miracles.

And God worked many miracles for this people. When the dust of the earth was turned into lice, this was a miracle. The magicians tried, but could not do it—their power failed. God turned the waters of the Nile into blood. He turned the Red Sea into dry land. He turned three days into three dark nights, when thick darkness covered Egypt so that no man saw his neighbor or rose from his place for three days. These were true miracles. Yet this people forgot God their Savior, who had done such great things for them in Egypt and wondrous things in the land of Ham.

And finally, terrible things in the Red Sea. Yes, even before the Red Sea, God did terrible things in Egypt. He plagued them in their souls, hardening their hearts. He plagued their bodies with boils. He plagued their crops with hail, their cattle with disease, their homes with frogs, their families with the death of their firstborn. These were terrible things. But the most terrible of all was at the Red Sea, when he drowned Pharaoh and all his host, so that not one was left. In this psalm you may see it: in verse 9, a work of power; in verse 10, a work of mercy; in verse 11, a work of judgment. The work of mercy was a great work. The work of power was a wonderful work. The work of judgment was a terrible work.

Yet for all this, see the unthankfulness of the people: they *forgot* it all.

But is it possible (you will say) that they could forget, in so short a time, all these works—that they did not remember them?

There is a twofold forgetfulness: there is forgetfulness of the mind, and there is forgetfulness in affection and in action. A man may have God in his thoughts, even on his lips, and yet forget him while he thinks of him, while he speaks of him.

I will show you by examples. Ask the idol-maker, Why do you make this image? He will say, to *remember* God by it. This is the common excuse of the Papists. Why have you these images? To *remember* God by them. But this is no true remembrance of God—this is to forget him. For when his commandment is forgotten, he is forgotten. His commandment is clear: "Thou shalt not make unto thee any graven image." They made the calf, thinking to have before their eyes a visible representation of God to remember him by. In truth, they forgot him then.

Or take the blasphemer, the profane swearer. He has the name of God continually in his mouth. He cannot speak three sentences without bringing up the name of God. But does he truly remember God, who swears by him at every word? No. This is to forget God. For if he remembered the name of God—that it is a good name—he would love it. If he remembered that it is a great name, he would fear it. If he remembered that it is a glorious name, he would reverence it. But he forgets that it is good, and great, and glorious; and so, even while he names God, he forgets him.

To conclude, let me make a brief application. If any nation under heaven may call God their Savior, next to Israel, surely we may. Consider how God saved us in 1588. Was not that a great work? Remember how God preserved us in the Gunpowder Treason. Was not that a wonderful work? Remember how God spared our lives from death only five years past, in that grievous and heavy plague. Was not that a terrible work?

And yet, brethren, have we not forgotten God? Have we not forgotten these works of his? Our falling from our first love, our turning again toward Egypt, our neutrality in religion, our faint hatred of idolatry and superstition—do these not testify against us? Add to them our pride, our wanton excess, our oppression, our false weights, our false oaths, our false faces. The ways in which we walk are so unworthy of the gospel of Christ that I fear God may truly charge us, as once he charged Israel: *They forgot God their Savior, who had done such great things, such wondrous things, and such terrible things for them.*

Sermon 5

Psalm 106:23, "Therefore he said that he would destroy them, had not Moses his chosen stood before him in the breach, to turn away his wrath, lest he should destroy them."

I have finished with the fearful sin of this people. I come now, in the verse that I have read, to show you the fearful punishment of God upon them for this sin: "Wherefore he said that he would destroy them, had not Moses his chosen stood before him in the breach, to turn away his wrath, lest he should destroy them." In these words there are two things:

1. The sentence that God pronounced against this people for their sin: *He said he would destroy them.*
2. The revocation of that sentence: the means whereby God restrained the execution of this judgment—Moses, his chosen, stood in the breach and turned away God's wrath.

First, *he said he would destroy them.* The judgment God threatened for this sin was not famine, nor captivity, nor bondage, nor pestilence, nor the sword of an enemy; but total subversion—the destruction of the whole nation. The words of God to Moses in Deuteronomy 9:14 are plain: "Let me alone, that I may destroy them, and blot out their name from under heaven." This was the sentence: to blot out their name from under heaven. As though God should say, I will never again be troubled with such an unthankful people. I will erase their very name from the earth. Not merely prune a branch from the tree, but uproot the whole. Not leave root or branch, head or tail. All of them together shall be buried in one grave of destruction. He said he would *destroy* them.

From this I set down one general proposition: Great sins—sins of a high nature, when committed with a high hand, with delight, with impudence, with impenitence—are enough to bring down God's judgment to the utter destruction of a whole people, of a whole land.

What are sins of a high nature? I told you before:

- Such as are directly against God:
    - Atheism.
    - Blasphemy.
    - Idolatry.
- Such as are directly against nature:
    - Sodomy.
    - Bestiality.
    - All incestuous and unnatural corruption.
- Such as are directly against human society:
    - Murder.
    - Robbery.
    - Rapine.
    - The shedding of innocent blood.

When sins such as these are committed openly and boldly, they bring not only ruin on households, as on the house of Jeroboam, or the house of Baasha, or the house of Ahab—houses which God swept away with the broom of destruction—but they bring destruction upon whole nations. They are able to lay the honor of the greatest kingdom, of the mightiest monarchy, in the dust, and that in a short time.

I need not stand long to prove it; a few examples will suffice.

For sins of this nature God brought utter destruction upon the world in Noah's time, leaving alive only eight persons. When the world was filled with such sins, it was then filled with water.

For sins of this kind God overthrew Sodom and Gomorrah, making that land a perpetual proverb of reproach. When God threatens final ruin, he says he will make it as Sodom and Gomorrah.

For idolatry, in 2 Kings 21:13, God threatens that he will wipe Jerusalem as a man wipes a dish, turning it upside down. In Ezekiel 21:27, he says of Jerusalem, "I will overturn, overturn, overturn it." And indeed three times Jerusalem was overturned.

First, by the Babylonian army under Nebuchadnezzar.

Second, by the Roman army under Titus Vespasian.

And then the very ruins of it were overturned again by the Emperor Hadrian. Titus had left it like a carcass, mangled and tortured, yet Hadrian left even the carcass so torn that, except for a turret or two and a fragment of wall, no man could say, *This was Jerusalem.*

Idolatry was first planted in the East; look now at the East. Where are those golden churches of Asia? Where are those learned churches of Greece? As Pope Pius II once said, a man may seek for Greece in Greece and not find it. They are all swallowed in Turkish tyranny and infidelity. For this sin of idolatry *God* overturned them.

In Leviticus 18 God sets out the sins of the people of Canaan—sins against God, sins against nature, sins against society. Then he warns Israel, in verses 25 and 28, not to defile themselves with these sins, "that the land spue not you out also, as it spued out the nations that were before you." It is a homely phrase, but a weighty one. As with a man whose stomach is burdened with meat that offends him, he can never rest till he has vomited it out; so, with a land overcharged with such sins—it can never rest till it has cast out the inhabitants that defile it.

The Spirit of God uses the same language in Revelation 3:16: "Because thou art lukewarm, and neither cold nor hot, I will spue thee out of my mouth." That is, I will cast thee out with loathing and indignation.

God is merciful, and his mercy is over all his works. But when sin becomes monstrous, God cannot forget his justice any more than he can forget his mercy. He must repay it in the end with vengeance. God may be provoked too far, and when patience is abused too long, it turns to fury.

When I consider the many sins under which this land groans, I name first what I named last: our lukewarmness, our neutrality in religion, our halting between God and Baal, together with our merciless oppressions, and our indulgent tolerating of vile dishonor done to the name of God. I do not wonder, brethren, that God has denied us this year his accustomed blessing in our fields. I do not wonder that he has so often sent us unseasonable weather. I do not wonder at the plague among cattle in many places. I do not wonder that the arrows of pestilence have flown abroad into so many corners of the kingdom, and drunk up the spirits of so many hundreds. I do not wonder at our mutual jealousies and discontents—perhaps the forerunners of heavier judgments. What I do wonder at is the mercy of God. Considering what a sinful nation we are, a nation laden with iniquity, walking unworthy of those high favors God has granted us, I wonder at his mercy—that we are not already consumed, that God has not blotted out our names from under heaven. Perhaps there are some "Moseses" in the land, some chosen servants of God, standing in the gap to hold back this judgment. That is the first point.

Now I come to the second. "He said he would destroy them; but Moses his chosen stood in the breach, and turned away his wrath, lest he should destroy them."

Here are three things observable:

1. A sentence of destruction pronounced against a people is revoked. God said he would destroy them, yet he did not.
2. One man—Moses, indeed a chosen man—procures this revocation for the whole nation.
3. The means by which Moses obtained this revocation: he stood in the breach, as God, like an enemy, had broken through the wall. Moses ran to the breach and stayed the hand of God.

Time will not allow me to handle all three fully. I will go as far as I can and leave the rest for another day.

The first point: the sentence is revoked. "He said he would destroy them."

If a man had said it, I should not have wondered that it was revoked. A man may speak and never mean what he says. "Man is deceitful upon the balance, lighter than vanity itself."

Or a man may speak and mean what he says, but lack the power to carry it out, as Sennacherib spoke proud words against Jerusalem. Surely, he meant it, for he came with a mighty army. Yet God put a hook in his nose and a bridle in his lips, and brought him back the way he came. He could not even shoot an arrow against it.

Or a man may speak, mean it, and have the power to do it, but then change his mind, as David did. He swore in anger that he would not leave alive a single man in Nabal's house. He surely meant it, and had power in his hand to do it; yet, by Abigail's wisdom, he was persuaded otherwise. He turned from his wrath.

But for God, the eternal truth, the very fountain of truth, in whom is no falsehood, neither deceiving nor deceived, for him to say and not to do? Balaam, though a false prophet, spoke truly: "God is not a man, that he should lie, nor the son of man, that he should repent. Has he said, and shall he not do it? Has he spoken, and shall he not make it good?" This is a weighty objection.

The answer is this, as Gregory said: *Deus mutare sententiam novit, consilium mutare nescit.* (God knows how to change a sentence pronounced, but he does not change his counsel.) His counsel—that which he has decreed and determined from eternity—is immutable, unchangeable as God himself. "With him there is no variableness, neither shadow of turning," (James 1:17). To be mutable is to be mortal; it is as possible for God to die as to change his eternal counsel. Yet he may change a sentence.

Examples prove it. God told Abimelech in a dream, "You are a dead man, for the woman you have taken is another man's wife." Yet no sooner had Abimelech restored her than God spared his life.

In Judges 10, the people were oppressed by Philistines and Ammonites. They cried to God for help. God answered, "No. I delivered you before, but you turned to other gods. Go, cry to them; I will deliver you no more." A fearful sentence. Yet when they repented, he delivered them again, and many times after.

Hezekiah was sick to death. God's word by Isaiah was, "Set your house in order, for you shall die." Hezekiah turned his face to the wall and wept. God revoked the sentence and gave him fifteen more years.

God sent Jonah to Nineveh: "Yet forty days, and Nineveh shall be destroyed." But though forty days passed, and forty more, and nearly forty years, Nineveh stood, for they repented.

How can this be consistent with the constancy of God? The answer is that God's threatenings are conditional. They turn upon repentance or impenitence, as a door turns on its hinges.

When God threatens to root out a people, it is upon two conditions.

First, that the wicked repent. Jeremiah 18:7–8: "At what instant I shall speak concerning a nation, to pluck up, to pull down, and to destroy it; if that nation turn from their evil, I will repent of the evil that I thought to do unto them." The sentence is pronounced absolutely, to strike terror, but it is intended conditionally. Though God does not change his will, yet he wills a change. If men know how to change their lives, God knows how to change his sentence.

Second, that his children intercede in prayer. This is what he looked for here. He said he would destroy them, but with this condition: he would not, if Moses prayed for them. Indeed, he encouraged Moses to intercede, saying, "Let me alone, that I may destroy them." Why say "let me alone," except to invite Moses to plead? "See, Moses, what power you have with me: I cannot strike if you pray."

Let me conclude with this *application*. There is a set period for every kingdom under heaven, sooner or later, as its sins ripen. Philosophers and divines alike have noted signs that a nation's ruin is approaching. If God seems now to threaten us with ruin, perhaps it is only conditional. There are two ways to revoke the sentence: repentance from the wicked, and intercession from the godly. O that we knew, in this our day, the things that belong to our peace! O that we might, like the Ninevites, humble ourselves and turn from our sins! O that Moses might again run to the breach, and with strong cries and tears beg pardon! For who knows if the Lord may yet be merciful to us, and turn his fierce wrath away, that we perish not?

I have shown the first thing: the revocation of the sentence—by whom it was procured (Moses), and by what means (standing in the breach). I must leave the rest until next time.

Sermon 6

Psalm 106:23, "Wherefore he said, he would destroy them, had not Moses his chosen stood in the breach."

I spoke the last day of the revocation of this sentence. I come now to the next point: who caused the revocation? Only one man—Moses. But Moses was a chosen man.

[Moses whom he had chosen.] Mark this: among God's elect in every generation there have always been some specially chosen men. Enoch in the old world was one—taken so that he did not see death. Noah was another—a man who found grace in God's eyes when the whole world perished. Abraham too, whom God called his "friend." Moses himself, with whom God spoke as familiarly as one man speaks with another. Elijah and Elisha were the chariots and horsemen of Israel. Daniel was dearly loved of God, "a man greatly beloved." Many more could be named. These are God's favorites, as dear to him as the apple of his eye, as precious as the signet on his hand.

Kings on earth have favorites; the King of kings has his. These are heaven's favorites, the "princes among men" (Micah 5:5). David called them "the excellent ones of the earth" (Psalm 16:3). One of them is worth a thousand others, for they have more power with God than many thousands. As the people said to David when he would go to battle against Absalom, "You are worth ten thousand of us," so may we say of these eminent ones. One Moses, standing in the day of God's hot wrath; one Phinehas, when the plague rages; one Elijah, in a time of drought; one Paul, in the midst of shipwreck—such men can do more than multitudes.

God's children are not always mighty according to the flesh. "Not many mighty, not many noble," (1 Cor. 1:26). Yet though poor and despised by the world, they may be mighty through grace. John the Baptist was contemptible in the eyes of men, yet the angel said he would be "great in the sight of the Lord."

Men of this world love to style themselves "great"—Antiochus the Great, Alexander the Great, Herod the Great, Pompey the Great. Yet the weakest saint has done greater acts than all these "great ones." Which of them commanded the sun to stand still? Joshua did. Which commanded thunder? Samuel did. Which commanded rain? Elijah did. Which of them ever stood in the breach against the great God of heaven and earth, turning away his wrath? Moses did. If one such man could *stay* God's hand against a nation, what might a multitude of God's chosen ones accomplish together, uniting their prayers for mercy?

The world, however, has never valued such men. They are counted the filth of the world and the offscouring of all things (1 Cor. 4:13). Job called them men of "no name." Paul calls them "things that are not"—that is, men who have no being in the esteem of others. Not only are they despised, but they are reckoned dangerous. Ahab called Elijah the troubler of Israel. The Jews of Thessalonica said of Jason and the brethren, "These men have turned the world upside down," (Acts 17:6). Tertullus accused Paul as a "pestilent fellow" (Acts 24:5)—the Greek says "the pestilence itself."

In the early church, if the Tiber overflowed, if the Nile failed to rise, if famine or pestilence struck, Christians were blamed. "The Christians are at fault—away with them, to the lions!" As if the world were not worthy of them. Yet Hebrews 11:38 says of saints wandering destitute and afflicted, "of whom the world was not worthy." Why not worthy? Because these men bring blessings to the places where they come. The world is not worthy of such blessings, nor of the men who bring them.

What blessings do they bring?

- By their presence. Jacob was a blessing in Laban's house. Joseph was a blessing in Potiphar's house. Elijah was a blessing in the widow's house at Zarephath.
- By their prayers. "The effectual fervent prayer of a righteous man avails much," (James 5:16). God promised Abimelech that Abraham would pray for him. He told Job's friends they must seek Job's prayer for pardon.
- By their example. They shine as lights in a crooked and perverse generation.
- By their influence on society. Paul's presence preserved all 276 souls in the shipwreck (Acts

27). Lot's presence kept Sodom from destruction until he was removed. If ten righteous had been found there, the city would have been spared.

- By their blessing on nations. "The righteous shall deliver the land," (Job 22:30). Even a whole country may be preserved for the sake of the upright in it.

In truth, the elect are not those who overturn the world—they are those who keep it standing. Were it not for the elect, God would have turned it upside down long ago. When the elect are gathered, then the world will end.

Let me *apply* this. If God shows favor to the wicked for the sake of the righteous, should not the wicked, for their own sake, show favor to the righteous? If Moses were gone, who would stand in the gap? If Aaron were gone, who would run with the censer and stay the plague? If the chariots and horsemen of Israel were gone, who would fight for us?

It has always been a fearful sign of coming ruin when many eminent persons are suddenly removed from a church or commonwealth. Methuselah lived until the year of the flood; only when he died did God send the waters. As soon as Josiah was slain, the captivity came on Judah. Isaiah 57:1 says, "The righteous perish, and no man lays it to heart; merciful men are taken away, none considering that the righteous is taken away from the evil to come." God takes them away because they would hinder him, they would run to the breach and stop his wrath.

Let me close with one more picture of Moses. In Exodus 17, Israel fought Amalek. Moses stood on the hill, lifting his hands in prayer. As long as his hands were raised, Israel prevailed; when he grew weary, Aaron and Hur held up his hands until the battle was won. Brethren, we should all be lifting up our hands to God for mercy. If you feel too unworthy, then do as Aaron and Hur—hold up the hands of those whom you believe God will hear. If you cannot act Moses' part, act Aaron's or Hur's.

Alas! the hands of God's children grow faint, they are discouraged, their knees weak in prayer. O, encourage them—lift up their hands. Perhaps God will yet hear and show mercy. So much for the first point: it was Moses who obtained the revocation of the sentence. I come now to the other, the means by which he obtained it: "*Had not Moses his chosen stood in the breach.*"

This is a military phrase, borrowed from war. If a city under siege is battered by engines, and a breach made in the wall, men of courage and valor run to the breach to stop the enemy from entering. So here: this fearful sin of the people had made a breach by which divine justice might have entered to destroy them all. Moses ran to the breach, placing himself between God and the people, that destruction might be stayed.

He stood in the breach in two ways:

1. By executing justice.

2. By interceding earnestly for mercy.

First, justice. When God's wrath burns like fire against a sinful people, there are two ways to quench it—two "liquors," so to speak:

- The blood of malefactors, shed by the sword of justice.
- The tears of God's favorites, shed in prayer.

Moses did both. He pleaded God's cause against the people with the sword, and he pleaded the people's cause with God by tears. In both he showed zeal—zeal for God's glory in one, zeal for the people's good in the other.

Consider his acts of justice. Though called the meekest man on earth, see what this meek man did when he found God's glory given to an *abomination*. He came down from the mount with the tables of God in his hands, and he broke them before the people's eyes—not in a rash passion, but advisedly, as Deuteronomy 9:17 makes clear, and with God's warrant. The people had broken the covenant; Moses broke the tables as a visible sign of that breach.

Next, he took the calf they had made, ground it to powder, cast it on the water, and made them drink it—so that their "god" might pass into their bodies and out again with their waste.

Still not satisfied, he cried, "Who is on the Lord's side?" The sons of Levi gathered, girded on their swords, and struck down three thousand idolaters—their brothers, fathers, and companions. With this blood the wrath of God was stayed. Never did Levi offer a sweeter sacrifice of beasts than this bloody sacrifice of justice.

When a sin provokes both earth and heaven, God's *justice* sets out against it, but slowly—waiting to see if man's justice will overtake it. If man executes justice, God's justice pursues no further. Jonah was cast into the sea, and the storm ceased. Achan was stoned, and Israel prevailed. Saul's sons were hanged, and the famine ended. Phinehas executed judgment, and the plague was stayed (Psalm 106:30). So too here, the blood of these offenders was poured out, and God's fire was slacked. Yet it was not fully quenched until Moses prayed.

Here is the second way—intercession. "The prayer of a righteous man avails much, if it is fervent," (James 5:16). Who can find a more fervent prayer than Moses made for Israel? See Exodus 32.

1. He reminded God of his propriety in this people: "Lord, they are your people." God had said to Moses, "Your people, whom you brought out of Egypt." Moses disclaimed them: "They are yours, Lord—will you lose what is your own?"
2. He reminded God of his mighty works: "You brought them out of Egypt with a strong hand." Shall your past mercies be wasted? Will you abandon the work of your own power?
3. He reminded God of his glory: "What will the Egyptians say? That you brought them out only

to kill them in the wilderness? Lord, will you let your glory be darkened?"

4. He reminded God of their forefathers—Abraham, Isaac, and Jacob: "Lord, these are their children. Did you love the tree, and will you cast away the fruit? Did you love the fathers, and will you now cast away their offspring?"

Then another argument Moses used was from the promise of God, confirmed with oaths: "You swore to them that you would give them the land. Shall not your promise stand? Shall not your promise confirmed with oaths be kept?" Here is his pleading for the people. As before, you heard how he pleaded God's cause with the sword, so here you see how earnestly he pleaded the people's cause with God. Yet, for all this, the good man feared, though God might turn from the evil, still he might not be fully reconciled to the people. So Moses went again to God with a vehement cry: "Lord, if you will pardon this people!" He said no more. But then he added: "If not, blot me out of your book." So intent was he on God's glory and the people's salvation, that he was careless of his own. "Lord, either forgive them, or blot me out." Such fervent prayer quenched God's wrath, which had been slacked already by blood, but was only fully extinguished by tears.

Scripture gives many more examples of men who stood in the breach. Samuel did; God himself joins Samuel and Moses together: "Though Moses and Samuel stood before me..." (Jer. 15:1). Ezekiel stood in the breach at another time. Josiah at another. God himself complains in Ezekiel 13:5 that the false prophets would not stand in the breach. And there is a remarkable place in Ezekiel 22:30, after recounting the sins of the people, and how those sins made way for justice to break in, God says: "I sought for a man among them that should make up the hedge, and stand in the gap before me for the land, that I should not destroy it; but I found none."

Mark that: "I sought for a man."

When sins have opened a gap by which judgment may come upon a land, God looks for a man to stand in it. He seeks someone to hold back his hand. Brethren, he who does not see what a wide breach the sins of this land have made—through which divine justice may rush in, and already has begun to break in—sees nothing.

Remember: did not God, only a few years ago, make us turn our backs more than once before our enemies? Did he not make us a scorn and derision to those around us? And now, does he not come among us, as Habakkuk describes, "with pestilence before him, and burning coals at his feet," (Hab. 3:5)? Do you not see, beloved, the swarm of new heresies in the world? New heresies daily broached, old ones revived. Do you not see the miserable rents and schisms in the church—some for Paul, some for Apollos, some for Cephas, some for all, some for none? Do you not see our divisions like the malignant aspect of planets? Is Christ divided? Do you not see the jealousies and discontents in the state? Surely God is looking for a man to come to the breach.

Help then, men and brethren—help, magistrates! It is *not* enough for you to weep over our miseries; you must put your hands to *redress* them. Are there no houses of correction for vagrants who live under no magistracy or ministry? No punishments for bawds, for harlots, for transgressors?

It is for us ministers too, to run to this breach. If ever we preached with power and demonstration of the Spirit, *it must be now*. O that we might be Boanerges, sons of thunder, crying down the sins that cry for vengeance!

And you masters, fathers, governors of households—run to the breach. If every man will sweep before his own door, the streets will be clean. Why do you suffer swearing, reveling, quarreling, drunkenness in your homes? Your houses should be churches for God. Where are your old household exercises of religion—prayer, scripture reading, psalm singing, catechizing?

I say no more. High and low, rich and poor, let us all run to the breach—by private intercession, by continual tears of repentance.

I conclude as before: Who knows whether the Lord will yet have mercy, and turn from his fierce wrath, that we perish not?

Sermon 7

Psalm 106:24–25, "Yea, they despised the pleasant land; they believed not his word: But murmured in their tents, and hearkened not unto the voice of the LORD."

Here we have two parts: the sins of the people, and their punishment. Their sins are set down in the first verses, their punishment in the latter.

Their sins were four:

1. Unthankfulness – "They despised the pleasant land."
2. Infidelity – the cause of their despising, "They believed not his word."
3. Murmuring – their old sin, "They murmured in their tents."
4. Rebellion – "They hearkened not to the voice of the LORD."

And their punishment was this: the Lord swore against them. Before, the text said, "The Lord said he would destroy them." Now, he swears it: "He lifted up his hand against them." Lifting up the hand was their form of swearing, and here God is said to do it. And what did he swear? That he would overthrow them in the wilderness; and not only them, but their seed also among the nations. Therefore, he punished both fathers and children: overthrown in the wilderness for the one, scattering among the nations for the other.

Now, that you may rightly understand these words, you must see the history at large which the psalmist here epitomizes. The full account lies in *Numbers 13–14*, with many profitable circumstances added in Deuteronomy 1:19 to the end.

The history *is this:*

Three months after Israel came out of Egypt, they arrived at Mount Horeb, otherwise called Sinai, for it was one mountain with two tops. There they remained almost a full year, departing only on the twentieth day of the second month in the second year.

At Sinai, Moses ascended the mount, received the law in fearful majesty, and remained there forty days. In that time the people made the golden calf. For that idolatry, God threatened to destroy them, but Moses stood in the breach and turned away his wrath. Moses then returned to the mount for another forty days and nights, received the ceremonial and judicial laws, and delivered to the people the pattern of the tabernacle with its vessels. Order was given for their march through the wilderness toward Canaan.

And mark this: before the law was given, God bore long with their provocations; but after the law was published, he bore less. At each station you find new judgments.

- At Taberah, they murmured, and God burned among them.
- At Kibroth-Hattaavah, they lusted for flesh; there the Lord smote the wealthiest and choicest

of them, even while the quail was in their mouths.

- At Hazeroth, Miriam was struck with leprosy for murmuring against Moses.
- Then they came to Kadesh-Barnea, on the very borders of the land of promise. Moses told them plainly: "You are come to the land which the LORD swore to your fathers; go in and possess it."

But the people, under pretense of prudence, desired spies first to search out the land. Moses consented, and God permitted it. Twelve were chosen—not men of mean rank, but princes, one of each tribe. Of these twelve, Joshua of Ephraim and Caleb of Judah are chiefly named.

Their instructions were:

1. Concerning the land—whether it were good or bad, fertile or barren, healthy or unwholesome, whether it bore trees or not.
2. Concerning the people—whether few or many, weak or strong, whether they dwelt in tents or cities, and if cities, whether walled or unwalled.

This was sound policy, so long as it was not mingled with *unbelief*. But here, indeed, their policy was mixed with cowardice and distrust.

In this way the men went, and viewed the land forty days. When they returned, they brought with them a branch of vine bearing a cluster of grapes so large that two men had to carry it upon a staff between them. They also brought pomegranates and figs, showing the richness of the land. All agreed in this testimony—that it was a wondrous good land, a marvelous pleasant land, as my text calls it. Joshua and Caleb, full of faith, encouraged the people: "Arise, let us go up and possess it." Caleb, whose very name means "hearty," spoke with courage: "Come, let us go up, for the land is worth our labor."

But the other ten, cowardly and faint-hearted, told another story. They began with praise: "It is a good land, flowing with milk and honey, just as God said." But then came the poisoned *but.* So men commonly speak: "He is a good neighbor, but..." Or as Scripture says of Naaman: a great man, mighty in valor, but a leper. So Papists commend the Scriptures—"a holy book, written by the Spirit of God, full of holy matter, holy style, holy end"—but, they say, it is too hard for laymen, therefore keep them from it; ignorance, they claim, is the mother of devotion. Just so did these spies: "Yes, it is a good land; *but* it is impossible to possess it."

And why? First, the men were giants, sons of Anak, tall as cedars, strong as oaks. "We were in our own sight as grasshoppers," they said, "and so we were in theirs." Second, their cities were fortified, walled up to heaven, they said; impossible to scale such walls. Third, they gave the land itself a bad report: "It is a land that eats up its inhabitants." Some suppose this meant pestilential vapors and plagues; some think it meant civil wars; others that the labor of tillage consumed the strength of men. Whatever the meaning, they slandered the land, making it sound hopeless to possess.

The people, hearing this, fell to their old sin of weeping all night long. If only they had wept for their sin of unbelief! But no, their mourning turned into murmuring.

- Against God: when God had said, "Because I loved your fathers, I give you this land," they turned it upside down: "Because the Lord hated us, he brought us out of Egypt to kill us."
- Against Moses: "Were there no graves in Egypt? Better to have died there than here in the wilderness!" They wished themselves dead for fear of death.
- Against the promise itself: they proposed to choose a captain and return to Egypt, refusing the pleasant land.

Moses and Aaron fell on their faces; Joshua and Caleb exhorted them: "The Lord who smote Amalek and Egypt will also smite the Anakim!" But the people would have stoned them, had not the glory of the Lord appeared at the tabernacle.

Then God swore in his wrath: of all that generation, six hundred thousand strong, not one should enter the land of promise, save Caleb and Joshua. Since they wished to die in the wilderness, so it would be; their carcases should fall there. He turned them back toward the Red Sea, to wander thirty-eight more years until that unbelieving generation was consumed. Their children would inherit the land, but not they.

And when at last they heard that God had sworn their exclusion, then in their stubbornness they tried to go up. God warned them: "Go not up, for I am not among you." Yet they went, and were smitten by their enemies.

So now the text is clear: "They despised the pleasant land, they believed not his word." The spies said one thing, God another. They believed man rather than God. They murmured in their tents—first against God, then against Moses—and finally refused the land altogether. And when God forbade them, then they would go. Therefore their disobedience was complete.

Now that the history is laid open, we may draw from these words the lessons they naturally yield.

I begin, then, with their first sin: their despising of the pleasant land.

The text saith they *contemptuously despised* it. So the word imports—a scorning, a loathing, as if it were vile. And this sin of theirs will appear more grievous yet, if you consider two things with me:

First, that it was indeed a *pleasant* land. To despise any land given by God in mercy, after deliverance from such a house of bondage as Egypt, had been evil enough. But to despise a land so pleasant—a land of desire, as the Hebrew calls it, a land that if a man might wish a country, he could not wish a fairer—that was sin above measure.

The Scripture everywhere sets forth its beauty. Let me, for a little while, unfold its pleasantness.

1. The situation. It lay in the midst of the earth, as the prophets say. Asia to the east, Europe to the west, Africa to the south, Persia and Armenia to the north. Psalm 74:12 says, "The Lord wrought salvation in the midst of the earth"—applied mystically by the fathers to Christ's cross at Jerusalem. God himself saith, Ezekiel 5, "This is Jerusalem that I have set in the midst of the nations." Again, Ezekiel 38:12 calls them "a people dwelling in the navel of the earth." And though our maps may not fall exact, yet all cosmographers agree—there was no land with easier passage to the nations of the world. The situation was most pleasant.
2. The air. Hotter than ours, lying some thirty-two or thirty-three degrees from the line, yet sweet and temperate, free from pestilent vapors, not subject to epidemical plagues.
3. The waters. It lacked great navigable rivers, yet abounded with brooks, springs, and fountains. Deuteronomy 8:7 calls it "a land of brooks of water, of fountains, and depths that spring out of valleys and hills."
4. The corn. It was a land of wheat and barley (Deut. 8:8). Though but one hundred fifty miles in length, and fifty to sixty in breadth, yet in David's time it sustained a multitude beyond

number—thirteen hundred thousand fighting men, besides Benjamin and Levi, besides women, children, and aged. Truly a fat land, rich in harvest.

5. The trees and fruits. Vines of renown, whose wine was prized among the nations. Fig trees, pomegranates, almonds, dates, olives—therefore called "a land of oil olive." Around the lake of Gennesaret the soil was so kindly, fruits of all climates grew together—such was its fertility.
6. Other commodities. The mountains yielded iron and brass (Deut. 8:9). From Engedi came the choicest balm. The lakes abounded with fish. And in general, God said it was "a land wherein thou shalt eat bread without scarceness, thou shalt not lack any thing in it." Judges 18:10 says of one city, Laish, "It wanteth nothing that is in the earth." Ezekiel 20:6 calls it "the glory of all lands."

Such was the land they *despised.*

But now ask—what is become of that glory? Of all lands under heaven, none ever smitten with so fearful a curse. Now it lies under the Turk. Where inhabited at all, it is by barbarous Turks in the valleys, wild Arabs in the hills. Much of it unpeopled, unhusbanded, desert. Travelers tell of goodly valleys overrun with rank grass waist-high, unmown, uneaten, perishing like grass on the housetop. Places once richest under heaven now lairs for lions, wolves, boars, and leopards. Fulfilled is the Psalmist: "He turneth a fruitful land into barrenness, for the wickedness of them that dwell therein."

And, brethren, let us not forget—we live in a pleasant land too. It is too long to name all the commodities of this nation. You know them well. Truly, your lot is fallen in a good ground, and you have a goodly heritage.

Let us then be thankful to this good God for the good land he has given us, and let us beware unless the pleasures of the land make us forget him. Mark it well: whenever God sets before his people the commodities of that pleasant land of Canaan, he adds a charge. "When thou art come into that good land... a land of brooks and fountains, of wheat and barley, of pomegranates, vines, and fig trees, a land whose stones are iron, and out of whose mountains thou mayest dig brass; when thou hast eaten and art full, then beware lest thou forget the LORD thy God," (Deut. 8).

It is an easy matter to forget God in plenty. *Too much abundance of good breeds too much occasion of evil.* The very mercies that should bind us nearer to God often make us cast him behind our back.

Take another lesson: let us take heed not to defile this good land. Were it never so pleasant—more pleasant than Judea, yes, Eden itself—if it is defiled with sins of a high nature, God's soul can take no pleasure in it. Remember David's solemn charge before his death to the overseers of Israel: "Keep and seek for all the commandments of the LORD your God, that ye may possess this good land, and leave it for an inheritance for your children after you forever," (1 Chron. 28:8).

So was it a fearful sin in Israel to despise such a land, first in respect that it was pleasant, and second in respect of the bondage where they came. They knew well the iron furnace of Egypt—how they were laden with burdens, scourged with blows, embittered in life, as Scripture saith. Yet they said, "O that we had died in Egypt!" To forsake the land of liberty for the land of chains—this was a sin abominable.

Had they despised it in regard of something better, it had been well. If a man despises even a fair and beautiful wife, because she draws him from Christ, he does well to despise her, for Christ says, "He that forsaketh not father, or mother, or wife, or children, for my sake and the gospel's, is not worthy of me," (Luke 14:26). Abraham, Isaac, and Jacob are commended for this—they confessed themselves strangers and pilgrims, despising Canaan in regard of heaven, seeking a better country, that is, a heavenly (Heb. 11:16).

But to despise Canaan in respect of Egypt, though fruitful and rich, yet a house of bondage from which God had redeemed them with a mighty hand and outstretched arm—that was intolerable. For this, God lifted up his hand and swore they should never enter his rest.

And is not this our sin too? God has promised us a country, a better country, a heavenly Canaan. We all confess its goodness. We say, "O what a glorious land is that! O how happy are they that are there!" Yet when we hear it must be won through battle—not against Anakim of flesh and blood, but against principalities and powers, the devil, the world, the flesh—then we draw back. When we hear we must forsake sin, deny ourselves, endure afflictions, then we despise that country, and prefer the Egypt of this world.

The worldling says, "Shall I lose my certainty here on earth for an uncertainty in heaven? Shall I forsake a sin that brings me profit or pleasure?" Therefore, earth is preferred before heaven, Egypt before Canaan, a mess of pottage before a birthright, swine before Christ, fleeting joys before eternal ones.

But the joys of that kingdom are unspeakable, endless, and full of glory. May the Lord, for his mercy's sake, and for Christ's sake, bring us to them.

Sermon 8

Psalm 106:24-25, "Yea, they despised the pleasant land; they believed not his Word: But murmured in their tents, and hearkned not unto the voice of the LORD," *etc.*

You have here the second sin—their unbelief: "They believed not his word."

That word was a word of promise, a particular promise of the land. God had said it; he had sworn it; yet they would not believe. The spies said it was impossible, and they believed the spies rather than God.

See the heinousness of this sin.

Unbelief was the first sin in the world. God said, "In the day ye eat thereof, ye shall surely die." The devil said, "Ye shall not die." Our first parents believed Satan, not God. Unbelief ushered in pride, pride brought in lust after forbidden knowledge, lust brought in disobedience, and disobedience brought judgment. Unbelief, then, lies at the root. And still, God cannot endure to be distrusted. If men, though liars by nature, cannot abide to be called liars, shall God endure it? Scripture says plainly, "He that believeth not God hath made him a liar," (1 John 5:10).

This people's sin was the greater because God had not only given his word, but had sworn with an oath. Among men an oath is the strongest bond of truth. Abimelech asked no more of Abraham than an oath. Jacob, in bargaining with Esau, asked only an oath.

Rahab asked no more of the spies. If men believe one another upon oath, shall not God's oath bind? Yet Israel would not believe, though God had bound himself with word and oath together. O happy people, had they believed! O wretched men, who would not credit even God upon his oath!

Greater still was their sin because they would not believe upon experience. They feared the Anakim, giants of the land; yet had they not seen what God had already done? Had he not drowned Pharaoh? Had he not fed them with bread from heaven? Had he not brought water out of the rock? And when water gushed abundantly, still they said, "Can he give bread also? Can he provide flesh?" The Psalm says, "The Lord heard this, and was wroth," (Psa. 78:20–21). It is unbelief upon experience that most provokes God. If a man trusts his neighbor upon long trial, shall not God be trusted upon his manifold mercies?

And now let us make use of it. It was not their sin alone; it is ours also. The best of God's children mourn daily over unbelief. Those that do not feel it are strangers to themselves. Look at one promise—"I will never leave thee, nor forsake thee," (Heb. 13:5). God said it, and he said it with utmost earnestness. In the Greek, five negatives are piled together, as if to say, "No, no, never, never, never will I leave thee." We may translate it, "I will never, never, never forsake thee." God never spoke more strongly. And have we not found it true? Twenty years, forty, sixty, some of us—never once has

God failed. In sickness, in want, in danger—*still* he upheld us. Yet how slow we are to believe!

You say you believe. Do you indeed? Then why the false balances and deceitful measures? Why the covetous tricks, the overreaching in trade, the restless cares, the sleepless nights, the neglect of worship, the forfeiting of sermons for worldly gain? If you truly believed God's promise to provide, you would never live so. As surely as the Lord lives, you did not believe it.

So it is with many other promises too. God has said them; we confess them; we experience them; and yet we stagger at them. O how slow of heart are we to believe! Therefore, we see that unbelief is not only Israel's sin—it is ours.

You see now the third sin: they murmured in their tents.

There is a threefold murmuring.

1. *Murmur displicentiae*—the murmur of displeasure, discontent against God, when things fall out otherwise than we desire.
2. *Murmur inobedientiae*—the murmur of disobedience against superiors, when their commands cross our own conceits.
3. *Murmur invidentiae*—the murmur of envy against our neighbor, when we begrudge his condition above ours. Therefore, the Grecians murmured against the Hebrews (Acts 6:1). In this way Cain against Abel, Judas against Mary's ointment, the elder brother against the prodigal.

But this text does not speak of envy; their murmuring was of displeasure against God, and of disobedience against God and magistrates.

See first their murmuring of discontent. Consider how often God spoke of the land to them as a gift of love: "Because he loved thy fathers, therefore he chose their seed," (Deut. 4:37). Again, "The Lord set his love upon you... because he loved you, therefore he redeemed you," (Deut. 7:8). Never people had more sensible pledges of divine affection. Did not his outstretched arm bring them from bondage? Did not the sea divide before them? Did not manna fall, and water gush from the rock? Did not the pillar of cloud and fire guide them? Did not God himself speak from Sinai, choosing them to be his peculiar treasure? Who could doubt his love?

Yet hear their voices: "Because the Lord hated us, he brought us forth out of Egypt, to deliver us into the hand of the Amorites, to destroy us," (Deut. 1:27). What monstrous misconstruction! To impute all tokens of love to hatred. Truly they were a people worthy to be hated, not to be loved, that could so interpret mercy.

Then, see their murmuring of disobedience. They cried, "O that we had died in the wilderness! O that we were dead!" They feared death, and in their fear they desired death. They might have lived, had they believed; but, because they feared to die, they wished themselves dead.

And mark how constant their murmuring ran. Forty years long God was grieved with their grumblings. When they wanted water, they murmured. When he gave water, they murmured at its bitterness. When they lacked bread, they murmured. When he gave bread, the very bread of angels, they murmured that they had nothing but bread. They murmured at Moses and Aaron's government; when punished for that, they murmured at the punishment. They murmured at the tediousness of the way out of Egypt; then, being shut from Canaan, they murmured because they could not return to Egypt. Like swine, whether full or empty, waking or sleeping, still grunting—so this people, whether in want or in plenty, in deliverance or in correction, still murmuring.

You have now the Apostle's warning—"This is written for our example, that we should not murmur as they murmured, and were destroyed of the destroyer," (1 Cor. 10:10).

Two lessons stand out.

First, beware of murmuring in disobedience. Children, beware of murmuring against parents. Servants, against masters. Subjects, against sovereigns. The Apostle says, "Do all things without murmurings and disputings," (Phil. 2:14). Chrysostom observes well—better no work done at all than done with murmuring. Murmuring is a muttering voice, low but sullen. It may be hidden from men, but not from God. Scripture says, "The Lord heard the voice of their murmuring," (Deut. 1). And the Book of Wisdom notes that the ear of divine jealousy will not let it pass. If for every idle word men must give account, how much more for words of murmuring against the Lord?

Second, beware of murmuring in impatience. Some cannot brook any cross. Let the weather turn, let providence deny some wish, and straightway they are set against heaven, charging God with hatred. But consider a few remedies.

1. Every discipline we suffer is from God. Affliction springs not from the dust. The beast submits to the keeper's hand; shall man rebel against his Maker?
2. God is righteous in *all* his ways. Though his judgments are sometimes hidden, they are *never* unjust. To murmur is to sit in judgment against God himself.
3. What you suffer may be less penal than medicinal. Poverty may keep you from pride; weakness may guard you from excess. God knows your frame and what state best preserves you. The Persians required that any man beaten by the king should thank him for remembrance. So should the child of God learn to thank the Lord for chastening, as a mark of his care.
4. Remember the *fearful* judgment on murmurers. God bore long with Israel. He endured their complaints at Marah, at Rephidim, at Taberah, and even Kebroth-hattaavah. But at last, he

swore in his wrath, they should not enter his rest. So, it is with all who persist. Gregory says well: "No murmurer shall enter the kingdom of heaven, but only the sons of peace."

Therefore, brethren, take heed of murmuring. It is a low sin in voice, but high in guilt. Let us rather learn contentment, thankfulness, and quiet submission to the hand of our wise and loving God.

Sermon 9

Hebrews 13:16, "But to do good and to communicate forget not: for with such sacrifices God is well pleased."

Concerning this sickness, this grievous sickness that now rages and reigns and spreads itself, more and more among us, just as we are not busy to seek a reason for it in natural causes, so we are not especially to seek the remedy of it by natural means. It is no hand but that of *God* that strikes us, and there is no hand but that of God that can heal us. It is no hand but that of God that gave the wound, and it is no hand but God's that must bind it up again. Therefore, it was a usual custom, both among the Jews and among the Gentiles, when the plague began to break out at any time among them, that the first thing they did was to seek to appease the wrath of God by sacrifice. The Jews did it by the light of grace, and the Gentiles by the light of nature. The sickness being now broken out, and for a long time, our course must still be to appease God's wrath by sacrifice.

Sacrifices in the old law were many; in the New Testament there is but one true, real, external, propitiatory sacrifice, that our blessed Lord offered on the altar of the cross, a sacrifice of a sweet savor to God.

But though there are none of that kind, yet there are sacrifices of another kind, a great number, by which we must seek to appease God's wrath. There are spiritual sacrifices, says St. Peter, "Ye also, as lively stones, are built up a spiritual house, an holy priesthood, to offer up spiritual sacrifices, acceptable to God by Jesus Christ," (1 Peter 2:5). And what are those?

There are especially *these five:*

First, prayer, that is a sacrifice. "Let my prayer be set forth before thee as incense; and the lifting up of my hands as the evening sacrifice," (Psalm 141:2).

The second sacrifice by which we should appease God's wrath is a contrite heart, that David speaks of: "The sacrifices of God are a broken spirit: a broken and a contrite heart, O God, thou wilt not despise," (Psalm 51:17). That is the second.

A third is a mortified body. "I beseech you therefore, brethren, by the mercies of God, that ye present your bodies a living sacrifice, holy, acceptable unto God, which is your reasonable service," (Romans 12:1).

A fourth sacrifice is in the verse before my text, a sacrifice of praise and thanksgiving. The Apostle calls it there *the fruit of the lips*, but Hosea, from whom the Apostle takes it, calls it the calves of the lips. Calves were once offered in sacrifice, and these calves of the lips ought to be offered to God, the sacrifice of praise and thanksgiving.

That God may be pleased in mercy to give us occasion to offer this sacrifice for our deliverance from this infectious and venomous disease, when it is His good will and pleasure, I have in the meantime thought it good to speak of a fifth sacrifice, almsgiving. "But to do good and to communicate forget not: for with such sacrifices God is well pleased," (Hebrews 13:16).

I do not need to divide the text; it divides itself into two parts:

1. An exhortation.
2. The reason for it.

"To do good and to communicate forget not"—there is the exhortation.

"With such sacrifices God is well pleased"—there is the reason for it.

Concerning the exhortation, I shall handle only that today, by God's grace. Consider *there:*

The matter, the thing we are exhorted to. And the manner, how the exhortation is framed.

The thing we are exhorted to is double, twofold: well-doing and communicating. "To do good and communicate." These are the things we are exhorted to.

For the manner in which the exhortation is framed, it is not simply, Do good and communicate; but rather, *Do not forget to do good.* It is a matter of great necessity: whatever else you forget, do not forget this. It is something you may easily forget: "to do good, and to communicate, forget not." And of these things, with God's help, I will speak with as much brevity and plainness as I can. I have many matters to go through, and I would be brief.

Mark first, I ask you, the two things we are exhorted to. They are substantives in the Greek. How they differ, or whether there is any difference between them, writers disagree. Some think they are both one and the same thing in two words. Others think the latter word is somewhat broader in extent than the former. The first word signifies an alms, or such relief as we give to the poor; that is, well-doing. The second word, communicate, includes under it all mutual offices of love and kindness that pass between man and man.

For the better understanding of what it means to communicate, let me first tell you this: just as different countries have their different commodities—as you know, one country abounds with good grain, another has good wine, another has good fruit, another has a good breed of cattle—so it is among men. Solomon had his oaks from Bashan, but his cedars from Lebanon, his fir from Shebar, his almug trees and gold from Ophir, his spices and perfumes from Arabia, his fine linen and horses from Egypt, his ivory, apes, and peacocks from Selvesia by his navy and fleet of Tarshish. Just as different countries have their different commodities, so different men have different gifts or blessings, which they are to communicate to others; just as every country through merchants communicates the commodities it abounds in to other countries, and in return receives other commodities that it lacks.

God would have one country stand in need of another for some commodity or other. So it is among men. God has so ordered His blessings that there is no man who does not stand in need of another. There is a necessity of both receiving and communicating.

Solomon tells us, "The profit of the earth is for all, the king himself is served by the field," (Ecclesiastes 5:9). The very king *depends* on farming. The citizens sometimes stand in need of the countryman, and the countryman at another time stands in need of the citizen. The poor man cannot stand in so much need of the rich man at one time, but that the rich man at another time stands in as much need of the poor. No member of the body can say to another, I have no need of you. As the Apostle tells us, "And the eye cannot say unto the hand, I have no need of thee, nor again the head to the feet, I have no need of you," (1 Corinthians 12:21). No, says the Apostle, those members that seem feeble are *necessary*. Those poor men, who may be contemptible in the sight of the world, are necessary. God has so ordered and distributed His gifts with such wisdom, that He would always have an exchange of kindness between man and man. There is a necessity of receiving, a necessity of communicating gifts.

Some men know how to receive, but they do not know how to communicate. Nabal and his servants received a great deal of kindness at the hands of David and his servants—they admitted it. David's servants were a wall about them by day and by night; they protected and defended them from all dangers while they were in the wilderness. But when David sent to Nabal for some relief at the time of Nabal's sheep-shearing, the churl said, "Shall I then take my bread, and my water, and my flesh that I have killed for my shearers, and give it unto men, whom I know not whence they be?" (1 Samuel 25:11). He knew how to receive kindness, but he did not know how to communicate.

As God has established a distinction of property among men, while every man governs his own house, rules his own servants, tills his own land, feeds his own cattle, and manages his own affairs, so every man experiences God's particular providence. As God has so established a distinction of property, of houses, goods, and land among men, so God on the other side has established a communion of saints. And the communion of saints does not abolish the distinction of property, nor does the distinction of property abolish the communion of saints. They may both stand together, the distinction of property and the communion of saints. God will have us, in regard to possession, to have things private and several as our own; but God would have us make these things common in regard to use, upon various occasions. Then a man does good when he communicates the good God has given him for the benefit of others.

Every man must consider with himself, in what way has God enabled me to do the greatest good? (just as Samson knew where his strength lay). And then to the utmost of his power, he must do good and communicate to others of that which God has given him. Forget not to do this, for with such sacrifices God is well pleased.

This doing good and communicating may be done in many ways. Mark them, because no one may be exempted from this precept of the Apostle. It concerns every man, and every man may do good and communicate in some way or other. We are forbidden to call our brother Raca, which in the Syriac means empty, worthless. "A man empty!" says Jerome upon that word—how can a man be said to be bare and empty, whom the Spirit of God has filled and endowed with some gift or other, that he may communicate, and in so doing perform good?

There are many ways of doing good. First, a man may do good publicly, or he may do good privately. He may do good to the Church and Commonwealth in general, or he may do good to some particular persons in the Church or Commonwealth. To distribute and to do good, both to the one and to the other, forget not.

For the first, to the public, a man may do good many ways. These especially come to my mind.

First, a man may do good to the public by building, enlarging, or adorning churches, chapels, and oratories for the service of God. A man may do good to the public by erecting and endowing schools and colleges for the education of youth. A man may do good to the public by making highways, causeways, and bridges for travelers. A man may do good to the public by bringing in water that may be useful either to city or country, and many other things. There are many more ways a man may do good to the public, and to do good to the public forget not, for with such sacrifice God is well pleased. For some such works as I have named, the memory of certain good men is blessed to this day, and will be hereafter from generation to generation, for such public works.

Then secondly, a man may do good to some particular person in the Church and Commonwealth, and that two ways:

1. A man may do good to the body.
2. Or to the soul.

The good that a man communicates may be either a bodily good or a spiritual good.

Then a man does good to the body, to the outward estate, when he communicates such a thing as is a means of his comfortable being in the state of nature. But a man does good to the soul when he communicates such a thing as may be a means of his well-being here in the state of grace, and of his eternal well-being hereafter in the state of glory. Now, to do good both to the soul and the body of your brother, forget not; for with such sacrifice God is well pleased.

I begin with the soul first, that is the principal part. Do you see your brother ignorant of some truth that he should know, which is necessary to salvation? You cannot do him a greater good than to *instruct* him. Do you see him doubtful what to do? Then do him good by *directing* him. Do you see him overtaken with some infirmity? Then *restore* him again, as the Apostle says: "Brethren, if a man be overtaken in a fault, ye which are spiritual, restore such an one in the spirit of meekness; considering thyself, lest thou also be tempted,"

(Galatians 6:1). The Greek word means, put him in joint again; he is out of joint, set him right, put him in joint with the spirit of meekness and gentleness. Do you see your brother unruly, rushing into sin as the horse into the battle? Then you may do him a great deal of good by admonishing and reproving him, to pluck him, as Jude says in his Epistle, out of the fire, that he perish not (Jude 23). Do you see your poor brother feeble and weak-hearted? Then you do much good by encouraging him. Do you see him dejected and cast down, almost swallowed up with despair? You cannot do him a greater good than to comfort him. These things you may do. And if you see your brother past all help from men, then you cannot do him a greater good than to pray and beg help for him at God's hand.

And indeed, that sweet communion of saints that we confess in the Creed—"I believe in the communion of saints"—appears in nothing more than in *doing good to the soul* of one another: to edify and build up one another in our holy faith, to exhort one another to holiness of life, to provoke one another to love and good works, to comfort one another in sickness, to mourn for one another's corruptions. This they may do when they are together. And then, pray for one another; and that they may do when they are a thousand miles apart. This is the communion of saints. In this way we may do good to the souls of our brethren; and to do this good to the souls of your brethren, do not forget, for with this sacrifice God is well pleased.

To the body we may do good, in the outward estate, many ways. I will note especially these three.

First, we may do them good *defendendo*, by defending our brother; by defending his person from violence, by defending his goods from ruin, by defending his name from reproach and dishonor. "If thou forbear to deliver them that are drawn unto death, and those that are ready to be slain," (Proverbs 24:11). Deliverance is one of the works Job speaks of among others: "Because I delivered the poor that cried, and the fatherless, and him that had none to help him. The blessing of him that was ready to perish came upon me, and I caused the widow's heart to sing for joy. I brake the jaws of the wicked, and plucked the spoil out of his teeth," (Job 29:12-13, 17). If you can do it in your calling, if your calling allows you to do it, you are bound to do it, to do that good, to right them when they suffer wrong, either in their person, goods, or good name. If it is in your power to right your brother, do good that way, defend him. That is one way.

Secondly, you may do good *accommodando*, by lending. Indeed, sometimes a man may do as much good by lending as by giving. And this is a work of mercy that God requires of His people. Mark that place: "If there be among you a poor man of one of thy brethren within any of thy gates in thy land which the Lord thy God giveth thee, thou shalt not harden thine heart, nor shut thine hand from thy poor brother: But thou shalt open thine hand wide unto him, and shalt surely lend him sufficient for his need, in that which he wanteth," (Deuteronomy

15:7-8). "Open thine hand wide" is the word; you shall open wide to your brethren, and shall surely lend to them. The original doubles it: in lending, you shall lend. That is, you shall surely lend, and lend sufficiently according to his need. So says the Old Testament. And Christ in the New Testament says, "But love ye your enemies, and do good, and lend, hoping for nothing again; and your reward shall be great, and ye shall be the children of the Highest," (Luke 6:35). And it is the commendation given to the righteous man: "A good man sheweth favour, and lendeth: he will guide his affairs with discretion," (Psalm 112:5). Mark the words that follow: "he will guide his affairs with discretion." That is the second way.

Thirdly, a man may do good *donando*, by free giving. Of what? Of that which is according to the necessity of your brother. If he is hungry, then you do good to feed him, to give him bread. If he is thirsty, give him drink. If he is naked, give him clothes. If he is sick, if it is in your power, give him a remedy. If he is dead, then give him burial, decent burial. Among the works of charity and works of mercy, you will always find reckoned in Scripture the burial of the dead. When Judas the traitor complained at the box of spikenard that was bestowed upon our blessed Saviour, Jesus said, "Let her alone: against the day of my burying hath she kept this," (John 12:7). And, "Blessed be ye of the Lord, that ye have shewed this kindness unto your lord, even unto Saul, and have buried him," (2 Samuel 2:5). What kindness? They buried his bones. It is a work of mercy.

In this way you see how many ways there are of doing good and communicating. A man may do good to the public in many ways. And then to the private, a man may do good to the soul or to the body: to the soul by instructing, directing, admonishing, reproving, encouraging, comforting, praying for them; to the body by defending them from wrong, by lending what is necessary, by giving according to their need when they ask. And therefore, to do good to the public, to the private, to the souls and bodies of our brethren, when it is in our power—forget not. It is a sacrifice with which God is well pleased.

Since there are so many ways of doing good, I will set down two corollaries and consequences. Two things follow from it.

The first is this: Since there are so many ways of doing good, certainly as long as we live here in this life, we can never lack opportunities of doing good in some way or other. That is the first. We cannot lack opportunities of doing good, there being so many ways to do it. Either a man will find some ignorant poor body whom he may instruct, as David did: "Come, ye children, hearken unto me: I will teach you the fear of the Lord," (Psalm 34:11). Or a man may find some person wronged, whom he may help and succor, as Job did. Or a man may sit at his tent door and find some stranger passing by whom he may entertain, as Abraham did. Or a man may find some fatherless children whom he may bring up, as Pharaoh's daughter brought up Moses. Or a man may find some naked person whom he may clothe, as Dorcas did. Or a man may find some wounded person, which, if he has the gift and skill of healing, he may heal, as the good Samaritan did (Luke 10:34). I could go further. It is impossible while you are here but that you will meet with opportunities of doing good. We cannot lack them.

Let no one excuse themselves with this, that they have no opportunity of doing good. They may have it daily, either to do good to the souls or the bodies of some, or perhaps both to soul and body. "I must work the works of him that sent me, while it is day: the night cometh, when no man can work," (John 9:4). The day is the time of life. We must follow our Lord in this work while it is day; while you have time now, here is the time to work good. The night comes; when death comes, there is no more time than to do good. "Whatsoever thy hand findeth to do, do it with thy might; for there is no work, nor device, nor knowledge, nor wisdom, in the grave, whither thou goest," (Ecclesiastes 9:10).

Think of that. You are going now to your grave. You do not know how long or how short a time it may be before you come there. Therefore, whatever your hand finds to do, whatever good God has enabled you to do, do it with your power; for there is no doing of good in the grave, where you are going.

Titus the Roman Emperor is commended by Jerome, and he deserved commendation indeed. Jerome sets forth his example and saying to others as worthy. Titus the Roman Emperor would every night call himself to account: what good had he done that day? And if he found that all the day long no good had been done, he would cry out to his friend, "Friend, I have lost a day." A great loss it seemed to him. But to us Christians, it is a greater loss, for we know we must *give account to God* for every day of our life, what good we have done in it.

And surely, considering within ourselves how much good God requires of us—first in our general calling as Christians, and then in our particular calling, according to the places we hold in Church and Commonwealth and in our private families—it is not good to lose a day. Every day, do something. As that painter would never let a day pass over his head without some line drawn, so we should never let one day pass over our heads without some good work done, some good work every day. Since there are so many opportunities of doing good every day, never let a day pass over our heads without some good.

The Scripture says of the devil that he stirs himself, and the reason is, because he knows his time is short (Revelation 12:12). How much more should we stir ourselves to do good, knowing that our time is shorter than his? "As we have therefore opportunity, let us do good unto all men," (Galatians 6:10). Now, as long as we live here, a charitable heart will never lack opportunity of doing good. We will still have opportunity to do good.

But when we are gone, there is no opportunity of doing good. There is no doing good after; then we are to receive for what we have done already, whether good or evil.

Excellently Origen, with which I will conclude this point, says: The six ages of our life are as the six days of the week; they are days to gather manna in. But the day of death—that is our Sabbath. There is no manna then to be gathered. It is no day to gather manna when we are dead; but then we shall eat that which we have gathered before. There is no doing good when we are dead, but then we come to receive for the good we have done before, if we have done it. Therefore, "But to do good and to communicate forget not: for with such sacrifices God is well pleased," (Hebrews 13:16). That is the first corollary.

The second is this: Since there are so many ways of doing good, there is *no man* exempted from doing good. There is no man but may do good in some way or other. Indeed, rich men must be rich in good works. They that have much goods must do much good. But there is no man so poor that he may claim exemption from doing good because he is poor. Hear what the Apostle says: "Let him that stole steal no more, but rather let him labour, working with his hands the thing which is good, that he may have to give to him that needeth," (Ephesians 4:28). See, the poor laboring man, that labors with his hands, must not be free from doing good.

John the Baptist, when he was asked by the people, "What shall we do?" said, "He that hath two coats, let him impart to him that hath none; and he that hath meat, let him do likewise," (Luke 3:11). Let him that has two coats—he does not say, Let him that has ten coats, or many coats, but he that has two coats—let him share with him that has none.

Our blessed Lord lived upon, that which good women gave him. You will see that if you look at Luke 8:3. There it is said that Mary Magdalene, out of whom he had cast seven devils, and Joanna the wife of Chuza, Herod's steward, and Susanna, and many others, ministered unto him of their substance. Christ lived upon what good people gave him. Yet out of what was given him, he was accustomed to give alms. You may see that from the speech of the disciples, when our Lord had said to Judas, "That thou doest, do quickly," (John 13:27). They did not know what he meant, but they thought he meant either to buy something needed for the feast, or that he should give something to the poor (John 13:29). Our Lord himself lived upon what was given him, yet out of that which was given him, he gave to the poor.

The Macedonians are commended by St. Paul for their great liberality, that although they were poor—yes, deeply poor, it was deep poverty, so the word is, "deep poverty," as the Apostle speaks (2 Corinthians 8:2)—yet they abounded in liberality for all that. You know the woman in the Gospel cast in only two mites into the treasury, but it was all she had. It was but a little money, yet it was great charity, a great work of charity, for it was all that she had.

When the cripple asked an alms of Peter and John as they came to the temple, they said, "Silver and gold have I none; but such as I have give I thee," (Acts 3:6). If you have no silver and gold to give, that you cannot give, yet give such things as you have.

The widow of Zarephath had no gold or silver to give the prophet; she gave him a cake. She lost nothing by it; you know the story (1 Kings 17:12–16). Our blessed Lord says, "And whosoever shall give to drink unto one of these little ones a cup of cold water only in the name of a disciple, verily I say unto you, he shall in no wise lose his reward," (Matthew 10:42). If you cannot do good with your *aera*—your money—that you have none to give, then do it *ora*, with your mouth. You may do good that way. You shall find some ignorant persons; instruct them. You shall find some doubtful, that know not what to do; direct them. You shall find some poor comfortless creatures; speak comfort to them, speak kindly to them, speak to their heart. Solomon tells us, "Pleasant words are as an honeycomb, sweet to the soul, and health to the bones," (Proverbs 16:24).

If you cannot do the good you would, yet be willing to do the good you can. Do what you are able to perform, and God will accept your willing heart, just as He did the willing heart of Abraham to offer his son, though he did not offer him (Genesis 22:10–12); and the willing heart of David to build Him a house and temple, though he did not build it (2 Samuel 7:1–13).

In a word, to draw to a conclusion, every man must give according to his ability, as God has enabled him. And God does not look for small things from rich men. In the sacrifices of the old law, in the voluntary freewill offerings, the Jews had this canon: that if a poor man brought a rich man's offering, God accepted it. For example, a pair of turtledoves or two young pigeons was a poor man's offering, and there was another offering for rich men. If the poor man brought a rich man's offering, it was accepted; but if the rich man brought a poor man's offering—if a rich man came with a pair of turtledoves or two young pigeons—this was not accepted. Every man must give according *to his ability*.

We are not lords of what we possess, but stewards and bailiffs; and the greater the stewardship, the greater the account. To whom God has given but one talent, he shall give account for one; to whom He has given two, he shall give account for two; and to whom five, he shall give account for five (Matthew 25:14–30). Therefore, as our gifts increase, so our account increases. According to the cost that God bestows on the ground, He looks for fruit. Of some ground it is enough if it brings forth thirtyfold; but of some ground God looks for sixty, and of some an hundredfold (Matthew 13:8). And those who have a great deal of goods—if they do not do a great deal of good with it—must look for a great deal of punishment. And however little goods we have, we must do good with them.

You will hear many say: If I had as much as such a man has, I would do a great deal of good. Yes, a great deal of good! But first, why should God trust you with a greater estate when you will not do good with what you already have? Why should your father put into your hands a greater stock, when you will not employ that little? Be faithful in little, and then God will increase it, as the widow's oil (2 Kings 4:1–7), and you shall have the blessing. "To do good, forget not."

You have heard the thing exhorted to; now the manner. *Do not forget to do it.*

In a word, I will not dwell long on it. It seems that we are very apt to forget to do good, unless we are called upon. Therefore, our Apostle (for I take St. Paul to be the author of this epistle), when he writes to Titus, the minister of the Church, says, "Put them in mind to be subject to principalities and powers, to obey magistrates, to be ready to every good work," (Titus 3:1). It is one of his charges. Put them in mind to do good. It is part of our duty before God, to put you in mind to do good, that you may not forget it.

In Galatians 2:9–10, you will find that the Apostles Peter, James, and John—the pillars among the Apostles—gave the right hand of fellowship to Paul and Barnabas, that they should preach to the Gentiles, and the others to the Jews. And there was nothing agreed upon except this one thing: that they should remember the poor, wherever they went. Whether it was Peter, James, and John preaching to the Jews, or Paul and

Barnabas to the Gentiles, this was covenanted and agreed among them—to remember the poor, to keep them in mind.

Therefore, people must not take it badly from ministers, if ministers are still calling on them to do good and to communicate. It is part of our duty to call on you, that you do not forget to do good. And I could use many arguments to persuade you always to remember to do good; but let me speak of this one thing, and then I am done:

That the God who forbids us to do evil, has commanded us also to do good. It is not enough for a man not to do evil; he must also do good. Innocence is a good thing, to do no harm. But innocence is not enough for salvation. It is not enough for us that we do no harm; we must also do good.

That God who forbids us to vex the stranger, commands us in another place to entertain strangers (Exodus 22:21; Hebrews 13:2). That God who forbids us to grieve the widow and fatherless children, commands us in another place to relieve them (Exodus 22:22; James 1:27). That God who forbids us to take the clothing of a poor man for a pledge, commands us in another place to clothe poor naked men (Deuteronomy 24:12–13; Matthew 25:36). That God who forbids us to do harm to any man, commands us to do good to every man.

That dreadful sentence, "Depart from me, ye cursed, into everlasting fire," (Matthew 25:41), will not be only for doing evil, but also for not doing good, "For I was an hungred, and ye gave me no meat: I was thirsty, and ye gave me no drink," (Matthew 25:42). And because you did it not to one of the least of these, you did it not to me (Matthew 25:45).

All the trees planted in the house of God are called trees of righteousness (Isaiah 61:3). They *must* bring forth *fruit*; their leaves must be for medicine, and their fruit for food (Ezekiel 47:12). There must be good. God cannot endure that we should grow unprofitable. Let every man take heed that he does not grow unprofitable, that no good comes of what he does. Beware of unprofitableness. The unprofitable servant is bound hand and foot (Matthew 25:30). The unprofitable chaff is scattered with the wind (Psalm 1:4). The unprofitable fig tree is cut down (Luke 13:6–9). The unprofitable salt is cast out and trodden under foot (Matthew 5:13). God cannot endure unprofitableness.

I will conclude with that place in Ezekiel 15:2–4. The Lord asks Ezekiel, "Son of man, What is the vine tree more than any tree, or than a branch which is among the trees of the forest? Shall wood be taken thereof to do any work? or will men take a pin of it to hang any vessel thereon?" The vine, if it bears fruit, is good and comfortable for God and man, as in Jotham's parable (Judges 9:13). But God means the unprofitable vine tree—if it bears no grapes, what is it then good for? You cannot make a hook or nail of it to hang a vessel on. You can do so with other trees, if they grow unprofitable. The fig tree, or the apple tree, or others, when they are unprofitable and bear no fruit, you can make a peg of them to hang a vessel on. But the vine—what is it good for? Surely it is good for nothing but the fire. From one end to the other of it, you cannot make a peg to hang a vessel on. So, either there must be grapes, there must be fruit, or woe and eternal perdition. "To do good, and to communicate, forget not: for with such sacrifices God is well pleased," (Hebrews 13:16).

Sermon 10

Hebrews 13:16, "But to do good and to communicate forget not: for with such sacrifices God is well pleased."

Here is an exhortation, and the reason to enforce it. The exhortation is: To do good, and to communicate. And then we truly do good, when we communicate the good that God has given us for the benefit of others.

We have finished the exhortation. We now come to the reason that the Apostle uses to enforce the exhortation: "For with such sacrifices God is well pleased."

He does not say, with such *works* God is well pleased; but, with such *sacrifices*. There are spiritual sacrifices: prayer is one, thanksgiving another, repentance another, and beneficence another. But the thing that is offered to God in all these spiritual sacrifices is the heart: a devout heart in prayer, a broken heart in repentance, a grateful heart in thanksgiving, and a tender, compassionate heart in beneficence. It is the tenderness, compassion, and charity of the heart that makes it a sacrifice to God, well-pleasing to Him, and accepted by Him.

Again, he does not say, this is a sacrifice that God requires (though He does require it too), but, *This is a sacrifice that God is well pleased with.* It is motive enough to persuade a good child to do this or that, if it is something that will please his father. It is motive enough to persuade a faithful servant to do something, to tell him, this will please your master. It is enough to persuade any good subject to do this or that, if you assure him the thing will please his sovereign. It is motive enough to a Christian heart, to persuade him to do good and to communicate, if he is assured that this is a thing God is well pleased with.

But yet it is not every work done, not everything that has in it the substance of a good work, that is pleasing to God. More is required than this, in order for a *sacrifice* to be acceptable to God.

There is something required in the doer, and there is something required in the thing done.

There is something required in the doer. First, he must be in Christ, if he will offer a sacrifice acceptable to God. Take these rules:

First, if the person of a man does not please God, his works can never please Him. "And the Lord had respect unto Abel and to his offering: But unto Cain and to his offering he had not respect," (Genesis 4:4–5). God accepted Abel first, and then his sacrifice. God never accepts a man's offering until He first accepts the man's person. Now God accepts no man's person, except in Christ. "This is my beloved Son, in whom I am well pleased," (Matthew 3:17). The Apostle calls Christ "the Son of his love," (Colossians 1:13). And there are none whom God loves, except He loves them in His Son, the Son of His love. That is the first ground.

Another is this: though a work is good as it comes from the Spirit of God, the author of all goodness, yet it cannot come through our fingers without being stained. "But we are all as an unclean thing, and all our righteousnesses are as filthy rags," (Isaiah 64:6). If God should be extreme to mark what is done amiss in our best works, who could stand? Even as the offerings of the children of Israel were called holy offerings, yet as holy as they were, there was some iniquity in them. But that iniquity was laid on Aaron; and when he bore the iniquity of all the other, the men and their works were accepted. So it is here: the works of a Christian may be good works—good in substance, because they are works that God requires at his hands. They may be good in the fountain, because they spring from the Author of all goodness. And they may be good in the end, because they are done to the glory of God and the good of our brethren. But still, just as some iniquity cleaved even to the holy offerings of the Israelites, so some iniquity clings to our good works, however good they may be. When that iniquity is laid upon Christ, "who his own self bare our sins in his own body on the tree," (1 Peter 2:24), then our persons and our works are graciously accepted, and all the iniquity that clings to our works is mercifully pardoned.

This is the first thing—what is required in the doer to make his beneficence acceptable to God.

But that is not all. There is also something required in the thing done. And I shall show you that, by

God's grace, in the remainder of the time. I shall lay it down in four rules.

The first is about the end. And you must not wonder that I begin at the end; for although the end is the thing last attained, yet it is the thing first intended. It is the first thing in a man's intention. Besides, God regards not so much *quid*, as *propter quid*; not so much what we do, as why we do it. A man may do good works for bad ends, and then he must not expect God to accept them. It is the end that commends the action. Now there are three bad ends of doing good works.

One end some set before themselves in doing good works is to make satisfaction to divine justice for the sins they have committed. The Apostle would have us do good works "for necessary uses" (Titus 3:14); but God never appointed this use of good works. Our good works may be tokens of our secret predestination; they may be foretastes of our future happiness. But to think that by doing good we can make recompense and satisfaction to divine justice, and appease the infinite wrath of God for sin—before which even the very angels cannot stand—is a senseless and graceless fancy. It tends much to the dishonor of Christ, and of that all-sufficient satisfaction that He has made for the sins of the world, when He offered up His flesh a sacrifice of a sweet-smelling savor to God (Ephesians 5:2). That is one bad end.

Secondly, some set before themselves another end, which is to merit eternal life by their works. Our countrymen, the English Papists—Rhemists by education, Romish by profession—often stand to it, insisting that good works are truly and properly meritorious, *ex condigno*, even of condignity. They say in their commentary upon Hebrews 6 that good works are so far meritorious that God would be unjust if He did not give heaven to our good works. He would be unjust if He did not reward heaven to our works. This is the only place where they can find the name of merit, only because the Vulgate Latin has it. And in this regard they take their stand to prove the doctrine of merit, upon that word merit.

Allow me to show you that good works cannot be meritorious. I will give you these reasons.

One principal condition in a meritorious work is this: it must be done by a man himself. How can a man be said to merit anything by a work that he himself does not perform, but another does it by him, or in him? Now you know, there is no good work that we do of ourselves—God works all our good works in us. Hear how the faithful pray in the prophet: "Lord, thou wilt ordain peace for us: for thou also hast wrought all our works in us," (Isaiah 26:12). Our new translation reads "in us," our old, "for us." The word in the original will bear either one or the other. Take it as you will—in us, or for us—God has worked the work. "Lord, thou hast wrought all our works in us, and for us."

First of all, it is from God's grace that we are enabled to do good works. Whatever works they may be, it is grace that enables us to do them. And then, when we are enabled, it is from grace that we are willing to do them. Both our ability and our willingness to do good are from God. See how the Apostle speaks in 2 Corinthians 8. He says there, I would have you know the grace that is bestowed on the churches of Macedonia. And what grace was that? You may see in the two next verses—nothing else but their willing bounty, even above their power, to do good. "For to their power, I bear record, yea, and beyond their power they were willing of themselves," (2 Corinthians 8:3). That was the grace bestowed on them: they were willing to do good.

So then, if we have ability to do good, it is of grace. If we have willing hearts to do good, it is of grace. If we do any good, we must shout as the people in Zechariah 4:7 and cry, "Grace, grace unto it." Grace in enabling us, and grace in making us willing too. All is of God. So if a man does a good work, he is more indebted to God for it. God is not indebted to him, but he to God for making him able; and he is indebted to grace for making him willing. He can merit nothing.

Then mark a second reason why good works cannot be meritorious. Merit is *opus indebitum*—it is a work not due, that a man is not bound to do. For a man can merit nothing by doing what he is already bound to do. He would transgress if he did not do it, but he merits nothing by doing what he is already bound in many bonds to perform. "Doth he thank that servant because he did the things that were commanded him? I trow not," (Luke 17:9). "So likewise ye, when ye shall have done all those things which are commanded you, say, We are unprofitable servants," (Luke 17:10). If we are to merit anything at God's hands, we must do something that we are not bound to do. But how far short do we fall in the things we do, of what we are bound to do? We are so far from doing more, that when we have done all we can, we are unprofitable servants. How much more unprofitable are we, says Jerome, when we fall short of *that which God has commanded*?

Thirdly, good works cannot be meritorious for this reason: there must be some proportion between the work that is done and the reward that is given *ex condigno*. Now, consider what that reward is that God has promised. Not according to the worthiness of our works—you must not think so—but of faith, of free mercy He has promised a reward. And what is it? Look in 2 Corinthians 4:17 and see what it is. The Apostle calls it "a far more exceeding and eternal weight of glory." "For our light affliction, which is but for a moment, worketh for us a far more exceeding and eternal weight of glory." Mark this. First, it is glory that God has promised as a reward. Secondly, it is more than that, it is a weight of glory. More still, it is an eternal weight of glory. Further still, it is an exceeding, eternal weight of glory. And even more, it is an exceeding, exceeding eternal weight of glory. Our English cannot carry it so far as the Greek. In the Greek it is, exceeding unto exceeding. The Apostle could not express it—it was so great. He said as much as he could: a glory, a weight of glory, an eternal weight of glory, an exceeding eternal weight of glory, an *exceeding exceeding* weight of glory. Now I ask you, what proportion can there be between a little poor temporal service that we do, and such an eternal, exceeding, exceeding eternal weight of glory?

I will say no more concerning this point of merit.

Let us never talk of merits. They were all lost in the first Adam; we lost all merit in him. Let grace alone reign in Christ. Let us say with Bernard, *Meum meritum misericordia Domini*—my merit is the mercy of the Lord. Let me have no merit, for merit would exclude grace. And, as he says, there is no place for grace to enter when merit has taken up all the room before it comes. Therefore, that is no right end.

Thirdly, there is a third end that some set for doing good, and that is, glory from men. Vain men seek vain glory. In this way did the Pharisees: they would do much good, but they would do it in such a way that they might be seen of men. And indeed, it is lawful for men to be seen doing good. Our Lord would have us so to do good that we may be seen of men, to let our light shine before men, "that they may see your good works, and glorify your Father which is in heaven," (Matthew 5:16). If you are afraid of spectators, you shall have no imitators. If there are none to see you, there will be none to follow you. It is lawful to be seen doing good, but men must not do good to be seen. For then they shall have their reward of men, and none from their Father in heaven (Matthew 6:1–2).

There belong two things to every good work:

1. There is the glory of the work.
2. There is the reward of the work.

The reward, God is pleased out of His free mercy to us in Christ to allow us. He allows us the reward, but not the glory of the work. That must be His own, and He will not give that to another (Isaiah 42:8). If we deprive God of the one, we must expect God to keep back the other. If we keep from Him the glory of the work, God will keep from us the reward of it.

These are bad ends of good works. We must not do them to *satisfy the justice of God* for sin, nor with the opinion of meriting eternal life, nor to be seen of men.

What then is the true end of good works?

Briefly, in one word: the end of all good works is the glory of God, in the good of our brethren.

And God's glory is such a thing, that we are born for that end—to set forth the glory of God. As the grace of God is our Alpha, so the glory of God must be our Omega. As the grace of God is the beginning from which all things come, so the glory of God must be the end to which all things must be referred: "For of him, and through him, and to him, are all things: to whom be glory for ever. Amen," (Romans 11:36). And we cannot bring greater glory to God, and to His holy truth and religion which we profess, than by doing good works. When men see our good works, and see how pitiful and tenderhearted we are, what bowels of compassion we have toward our poor afflicted brethren, they cannot choose but glorify God, and acknowledge and say, "Surely they are the seed which the Lord hath blessed," (Isaiah 61:9).

So much concerning the first rule that I give you. Would you make your beneficence and good works toward your poor visited brethren pleasing and acceptable to God? Do them to a right end—to God's glory, and your brethren's good.

I come now to a second rule. The former was about the end; the second is about the fountain from which our good works must flow. And what is that? Compassion. If we would make our good works pleasing and acceptable to God, they must flow out of a pitiful heart. If you instruct an ignorant man, which is a good work, it must be out of pity for his ignorance. If you feed a hungry man, it must be out of pity for his misery. The distribution of our goods to the poor is accounted a work of charity—and so it is, a great work of charity. If a man should do as Zacchaeus offered, "Behold, Lord, the half of my goods I give to the poor; and if I have taken any thing from any man by false accusation, I restore him fourfold," (Luke 19:8), you would count that a great work of charity. But suppose a man should give all his goods to the poor, you would say that was a transcendent work of charity. And indeed it is so. Yet see, a man may do even this transcendent work of charity, and still have no charity. Mark the Apostle's speech: "And though I bestow all my goods to feed the poor, and have not charity, it profiteth me nothing," (1 Corinthians 13:3). See, a man may give all that he has to the poor, and yet have no charity—because what he gives does not come from a charitable, compassionate heart.

Holy Job does not only tell of his works of charity, but he tells also out of what ground he did those works of charity, out of what fountain they flowed. And what was that? His compassion. "Did not I weep for him that was in trouble? was not my soul grieved for the poor?" (Job 30:25). The works that a man does, if he would make them a pleasing and acceptable sacrifice to God, must come out of a fellow-feeling of his brethren's necessities.

It is said of our blessed Saviour in the Scriptures, He went about *doing* good (Acts 10:38). It is true, His whole life was nothing else but going about, doing good. And mark, you shall find in the Gospel that many of His works of charity are expressly noted to have come from compassion. Let me give some examples.

Our blessed Lord cleansed lepers, and it was out of compassion that He cleansed them: "And Jesus, moved with compassion, put forth his hand, and touched him, and saith unto him, I will; be thou clean," (Mark 1:41). In another place, when they brought many sick to Him, "he was moved with compassion toward them, and he healed their sick," (Matthew 14:14). Again, you know the miracle when our Lord fed four thousand men, besides women and children, with a few loaves and fishes. Why did He do it? Out of compassion: "I have compassion on the multitude, because they continue with me now three days, and have nothing to eat," (Matthew 15:32). Again, our blessed Savior touched the eyes of two blind men, and they received their sight. And it was out of compassion: "So Jesus had compassion on them, and touched their eyes, and immediately their eyes received sight, and they followed him," (Matthew 20:34). One more place: our Lord raised the young man of Nain, who was dead and carried out to burial. He touched the coffin and raised him again to life. Why? Out of compassion—not to the young man (for his estate might have been happier), but to his mother: "And when the Lord saw her, he had compassion on her, and said unto her, Weep not," (Luke 7:13). And He restored her son to life.

Mark also that phrase in Isaiah 58:10: "If thou draw out thy soul to the hungry." He does not say, *If thou draw out thy purse, though that is something; or thy meat from thy cupboard, or thy garments from thy chest, and give to a poor wretch.* But, *If thou draw out thy soul.* The soul must be drawn out first. And if a man once draws out his soul to a poor wretch, he will also draw out his purse, if he has it. He cannot but draw out his purse, if first he has drawn out his soul. Therefore, John says, "But whoso hath this world's good, and seeth his brother have need, and shutteth up his bowels of compassion from him, how dwelleth the love of God in him?" (1 John 3:17).

And while I name the bowels of compassion, let me tell you that word where it is said that Christ was "moved with compassion" is in the Greek σπλαγχνίζομαι (*splagchnizomai*). We cannot express it in one English word. It is from the bowels, meaning a deep inward motion. Beza renders it "the yearning of the bowels." So the bowels must yearn in us. When we see poor miserable wretches, we must not only relieve them, but relieve them out of pity and compassion, with tenderness of heart toward their misery.

If we would have our sacrifice of beneficence acceptable and pleasing to God, there are two things in doing good: the inward affection of the heart, and the outward act of the hand. These should not be parted, but go together—not only the inward affection of the heart, but also the outward act of the hand; nor only the outward act of the hand, but it must proceed from the inward affection of the heart.

Yet I can tell you one case where God accepts the inward affection without the outward act. Sometimes God does not enable a man to give a gift; then He accepts the good affection, a pitiful heart toward our brethren. Where God does not find ability to perform, He accepts a willing, loving, tender, charitable heart. He accepts the inward affection. But I cannot tell you any case where God accepts the outward action without the inward affection. The outward act of the hand may be more acceptable to the needy man who receives it; but the inward affection is what makes it a sacrifice pleasing and acceptable to God.

That is my second rule.

I come now to the third and fourth, which I will touch briefly. The third rule concerns the matter and substance of good works. Good works must be done with what is our own. It is a sacrifice we find here, and we must not offer in sacrifice to God what is not ours.

In 1 Chronicles 21:24, David came to Araunah the Jebusite to buy his threshing floor, to make an altar to God. Araunah bountifully offered him, "Take it, my lord the king, and offer what is good in his eyes: lo, I give thee the oxen also for burnt offerings, and the threshing instruments for wood, and the wheat for the meat offering; I give it all." But David said, "Nay; but I will verily buy it for the full price: for I will not take that which is thine for the LORD, nor offer burnt offerings without cost." David would not offer to God anything that cost him nothing. We may not offer to God what cost us nothing, but that which cost us labor, industry, and the sweat of our brows. What we have gotten by honest labor in our calling, let that come, and it is welcome to God. God cannot be pleased with a mocking sacrifice. And who among us would be content to be mocked?

The son of Sirach tells us, "He that sacrificeth of a thing wrongfully gotten, his offering is ridiculous; and the gifts of unjust men are not accepted" (Ecclus. 34:18). Such a sacrifice is a mocking sacrifice. And will God be mocked? Gregory said well, even we ourselves would not endure it. Whatsoever in our sacrifice is ill-gotten, it is so far from appeasing the wrath of God, that it provokes Him much more.

It is notable that in Scripture our alms deeds are called *righteousness.* Our beneficence is called righteousness in many places. "He hath dispersed, he hath given to the poor; his righteousness endureth for ever," (Psalm 112:9). That is, his alms deeds. And the Apostle prays for the Corinthians, "Being enriched in every thing to all bountifulness, which causeth through us thanksgiving to God… being fruitful in every good work, and increasing the fruits of your righteousness," (2 Corinthians 9:11, 10). That is, their beneficence. Beneficence is called righteousness.

And that which we read in Matthew 6:1, "Take heed that ye do not your alms before men, to be seen of them"—the Vulgate Latin reads, "Take heed that ye do not your righteousness before men." Beza reads it so too, and he says that in two of the most ancient Greek copies he had, it was so. The Syriac interpreter also reads it thus: "Take heed that ye do not your righteousness before men."

I will add this also: Christ Himself looked on those who cast money into the treasury. And what was that treasury? It was a chest at the door (as your poor man's box), into which they were accustomed to cast money as they passed by out of the temple. And this the

Hebrews called the *chest of righteousness*. Not the chest of mercy, nor of charity, but of *righteousness*.

Why should our alms deeds be called righteousness?

I could give you many reasons, but let this suffice at this time, because God would have that to be righteously brought in, which is charitably laid out. We must lay out nothing charitably, except what has first been righteously brought in. What is laid out for good uses must first be gotten by good means. Let it be righteously gotten, and then it will be a sacrifice pleasing and acceptable to God. That is my third rule: it must be our own that we give.

The fourth and last rule, which I will only name to you, is this: about the manner. It must be done cheerfully. The first rule was about the end—it must be done to a good end. The second rule was about the fountain from which it must flow—a pitiful heart. The third rule was about the matter or substance—it must be our own. The last rule is about the manner—it must be done with alacrity and cheerfulness.

And this cheerfulness must appear, first, in the countenance. A man must not give with an angry, unwilling countenance.

Then it must appear in the words of a man. For a man may perhaps undo a good work with ill words. He may bring a blemish on a good work with ill words. "Pleasant words are as an honeycomb, sweet to the soul, and health to the bones," (Proverbs 16:24). As there must be compassion and bowels, so there must be grace and favor in the lips. A good word sometimes may do more good than a good deed, to cheer and comfort a poor soul and revive it.

Thirdly, our cheerfulness must be shown by our speedy giving. He gives twice, that gives quickly. A man blemishes his good work if he delays it. So much is taken away from the worth of every work, as much as it sticks longer in the fingers of he that does it.

Now you see, brethren, how you may make good works pleasing and acceptable to God. Your persons must first be in Christ. Then you must have *a good end.* You must not set before yourselves to make satisfaction to divine justice, or to merit eternal life, or to think thereby to be seen of men for vainglory and popularity. But your end must be God's glory, and your brethren's good. And then this must flow out of a pitiful heart: "He that despiseth his neighbour sinneth: but he that hath mercy on the poor, happy is he", (Proverbs 14:21). He does not say, He that gives to the poor; yet he would not have it a barren, fruitless pity. The meaning is this: he that pities the poor and gives out of pity, happy is he. Then again, it must be your own that you give. It must not be a burnt offering of goods gotten by robbery or unjust means.

Then lastly, it must be done with cheerfulness—cheerfulness shown in the countenance, in words, in speediness and readiness to give. If it is done this way, then it is a sacrifice acceptable to God.

No, I will go further: God will reward such a sacrifice as this. You shall be sure of a reward at the hand of God, though not for the merit of the work (away with merit, talk not of that). Yet you shall have a reward, through the free mercy of God in Christ.

You say, that is lost which is bestowed on an unthankful person. But, as Luther says, if a man will not do good unless he can find a thankful man, let him look for another world to do it in, for this is not the world for him. If one of ten gives thanks, it is enough. It was so with Christ: of ten lepers healed, one returned to give thanks (Luke 17:17–18). Yet though men prove unthankful, though they do not seem to repay, though men forget, yet our good God will not forget. Hear what the prophet says: "Bring ye all the tithes into the storehouse, that there may be meat in mine house, and prove me now herewith, saith the Lord of hosts, if I will not open you the windows of heaven, and pour you out a blessing, that there shall not be room enough to receive it," (Malachi 3:10). Try me now, says the Lord. Beloved brethren, you have tried many men, and you have made ventures, some perhaps to the farthest parts of the world, some within this kingdom. And you dare trust this man and that man with your estates and goods, and perhaps some have cheated you of much. Man is deceitful on the balances, lighter than vanity itself. But trust God with something. Venture something to heaven. You venture in giving to the poor. You think it is a hazard. But you never make so safe a return of any commodity in the world, as of that which you give to your brethren.

Riches we call the muck of the world. I wish we thought of it as we call it—the muck of the world. May I give you a comparison? A heap of muck, as it lies in the yard, does no good. But carry it abroad into your pasture fields and spread it, and you find the benefit of it. So it is with your money and your goods. As long as they lie heaped up with you, they do no good. Carry them abroad and disperse them. As the Scripture says, "He hath dispersed, he hath given to the poor," (Psalm 112:9). It is taken from dung spread in the field. Lay it out upon your poor brethren, and look for an increase. If you do not receive it in this life, be assured you shall have it in the life to come. If not in outward blessings, yet you shall be enriched in grace here, and in glory hereafter.

To which the Lord bring you, for His sake who has dearly purchased it for you, Jesus Christ the righteous. Amen.

Sermon 11

A SERMON PREACHED at Pauls, November 14th, 1641.

2 Cor. 6:8, "By honour and dishonour, by evil report and good report, as deceivers and yet true."

The words refer to the fourth verse, in which the blessed vessel of election, Saint Paul, begins to show how he, and Timothy, and other faithful ministers of Jesus Christ, approved themselves to be so—by patience, by purity, by knowledge, by longsuffering, by kindness, by the Holy Spirit, by love unfeigned, by the Word of truth, by the power of God, by the armor of righteousness on the right hand and on the left. And all this, when (as it is in the text) they passed through honor and dishonor, evil report and good report, accounted to be deceivers when they were true.

In handling the words (in which are three antitheses), I will take this course: First, to handle the antitheses themselves severally. Second, to show how it is the lot of the best of God's children to pass through every one of them. Third, to show that we shall then approve ourselves to be true ministers of Jesus Christ (as Saint Paul does here), when—passing through honor and dishonor, evil report and good report, held to be deceivers when we are yet true—we nonetheless keep the faith, hold our ground, and fulfill our ministry.

Honor, in Greek, is nothing else but a good opinion and estimation, found among those that are wise, virtuous, and religious—arising from the acknowledgment either of some grace with which God has honored a man, or of some virtuous action by which that man has honored God. And this honor is shown not only by salutations and greetings in the marketplace, which pleased the Pharisees; nor only in titles, to be called Rabbi, Rabbi, which they loved; but in the performance of good offices, observances, and rewards, which are therefore called honoraria, as given by way of honor. As the Queen of Sheba honored Solomon with one hundred and twenty talents of gold, besides spices and precious stones (1 Kings 10:10). As the men of Judah honored Jehoshaphat with so many presents that he had riches and honor in abundance (2 Chronicles 17:5). So the wise men honored Christ not only by worshipping Him, but also by presenting Him with gold, frankincense, and myrrh (Matthew 2:11). Paul himself, with his companions, was honored with many honors, says Luke (Acts 28:10).

And what is that "double honor" which elders that rule well are worthy of (1 Timothy 5:17), but reverence and maintenance? If maintenance is taken away, reverence is soon lost. "The wisdom of the poor man is despised, and his words are not heard," (Ecclesiastes 9:16).

This honor must be acknowledged as a blessing from God, *both* a reward for former good service and an encouragement for future faithfulness. In this way Abraham, though a stranger, was honored by the Hittites as a prince of God, and given his choice among their sepulchers (Genesis 23). Jehoiada, that reverend high priest, lived and died with honor, being buried among the kings because he had done good in Israel, toward God and His house (2 Chronicles 24:16). And John the Baptist, though living a solitary life, lacked not honor among the people, who counted him a prophet, nor even with Herod, who feared him because he was a just and holy man.

Goodness may command honor, when greatness must beg for it. Honor nourishes arts: learning would quickly decay if honor were taken away from it. Honor encourages to virtuous actions—*Virtutis uberrimum nutrimentum honos*, honor is the greatest nourishment of virtue. Honor puts men upon the greatest services: David dared to fight Goliath, after he had heard how the man should be honored that slew him.

There is no noble spirit that does not value honor highly. Many in history—Ajax, Brutus, Antony, Cato, and others—chose death rather than dishonor. So did Saul, falling upon his own sword; so did Samson, pulling the house down upon himself and the Philistines. Abimelech was more troubled at dying dishonorably, by the hand of a woman, than at dying itself (Judges 9:54). What has caused so many duels and quarrels among men of spirit, but a too tender sense of wrongs done to their honor?

Even God's children have felt this deeply. Elisha could not bear to be dishonored by *mocking children*. Job complained most bitterly of scorn and contempt, which he endured from men he would once have disdained to set with the dogs of his flock (Job 30). Nehemiah prayed against reproaches cast upon God's people: "Hear, O our God, for we are despised," (Nehemiah 4:4). The people cried in the Psalms, "Have mercy upon us, O Lord, for we are exceedingly filled with contempt," (Psalm 123:3–4).

And what was one of the bitterest ingredients in the cup our Lord drank? Shame and dishonor. "I am a worm, and no man; a reproach of men, and despised of the people," (Psalm 22:6). The cross was as much about shame as about pain, yet Christ "endured the cross, despising the shame, and is set down at the right hand of the throne of God," (Hebrews 12:2). If we would reign with Him, we must be willing to suffer with Him, and to bear the contempt of the world for His cause, resolving with David, "I will yet be more vile than thus," (2 Samuel 6:22).

The next antithesis is *good report* and *evil report*. A good report is precious. Yet three cautions must be *given:*

First, we must not expect it from all men. "Woe unto you, when all men shall speak well of you," (Luke 6:26). It is enough to be well reported of by the best.

Second, we must not expect it always from the mouths of men. "We commend ourselves to every man's conscience in the sight of God," (2 Corinthians 4:2).

Their consciences may approve, when their lips withhold a good word.

Third, we must not expect it at *all* times. A good report may hurt us if it feeds our pride, and an ill report may do us good if it humbles us or makes us more wary. But a good report from the mouths of the godly, or from the consciences of the wicked at times when it brings honor to God, is one of life's greatest blessings.

It is a *bonum utile*, useful, a second patrimony. "A good name is rather to be chosen than great riches," (Proverbs 22:1). It is a *bonum jucundum*, pleasant: "A good name is better than precious ointment," (Ecclesiastes 7:1). It draws others, as ointment draws pigeons to the dovehouse. So, Christ's name is "ointment poured forth" (Song of Solomon 1:3). A preacher of good report shall not want hearers; a physician shall not want patients; a tradesman shall not want customers. It is a *bonum honestum*, honest and virtuous. Among the things to be thought on are "whatsoever things are of good report," (Philippians 4:8).

In this way the child of God must not only keep a good conscience before God, but also a good name before men: "Providing for honest things, not only in the sight of the Lord, but also in the sight of men," (2 Corinthians 8:21). Bernard said well: in the lily are whiteness and sweetness—so must a Christian have the candor of conscience and the fragrance of a good name. My conscience is for myself, but my good name is for others.

This is why deacons were required to have "honest report" (Acts 6:3), widows to be "well reported of for good works" (1 Timothy 5:10), and bishops to have "a good report of them which are without" (1 Timothy 3:7). For an evil report upon a minister stains the ministry, and an evil report upon a professor dishonors the gospel. Better to die than to live to bring shame upon the name of Christ.

And since these are days filled with evil reports, when men cast cartloads of reproaches into one another's faces, let me briefly show what good use may be made of evil reports.

First, let us examine our consciences, whether they are true or not. If they are altogether false, then we may comfort ourselves in the testimony of a good conscience; and if our adversaries should write a book against us (and there are books enough written on that argument, cried every day up and down our streets), we might, with holy Job, take it upon our shoulders, and bind it as a crown to our heads (Job 31:35–36). But if the reports are in any part true, then it is fitting that we should lie down in our shame, give God the glory of His justice, beg mercy, bear the punishment with patience, and give Him thanks for it: "I will bear the indignation of the Lord, because I have sinned against him," (Micah 7:9).

If the reports are not altogether true, then let us search the wound a little deeper, and see whether we have not given just occasion for such a report. It was said of that Vestal Virgin, *Casta quidem, sed non est credita,*[5] she was indeed chaste, but not thought to be so, because she was more wantonly attired than became such a virgin. It may be, though we are not as bad as we are reported to be, yet upon examination we may find we are not as good as we ought to be, in shunning the occasions and appearances of evil. That alone should be sufficient matter for humiliation. If we are free from giving occasion, yet we should do well to search deeper still, and see whether we have not entertained some morose cogitations and thoughts of that very sin with which we stand charged by report. It may be that wickedness has been sweet in our mouths, and we have rolled it under our tongues (Job 20:12). Though we have not swallowed it down, yet perhaps we have not spit it out. And then, though *cogitationis poenam nemo patitur*[6]—no man is punished for his thoughts by the law of men—yet it is a righteous thing with God, the Searcher of hearts, to punish that sin, which has found such kind entertainment, by false reports, or to punish us for some other sin in which we have continued without repentance.

Lastly, it may please God in mercy that such a false report should be charged upon us unjustly, that we may be more careful of our ways, and watchful over our hearts, with a holy jealousy against that sin, unless we be justly charged with it another day. Good God, teach

[5] Ovid, Fasti, lib. 4.

[6] Digest. lib. 48, tit. 19, de Poenis.

us to make this good use of evil reports. And so, I have done with evil reports in general, and come now to one evil report in particular, which cannot but much trouble a true servant of God—to be counted a deceiver, when he is true.

"As deceivers," says the Apostle, "and yet true," (2 Corinthians 6:8). *Ut Seductores, et tamen Veraces*, there is no liar who would willingly be accounted a liar. We see how ready some are, even while lying, to present death upon the point of a sword to the man that shall give them the lie. There are no false prophets—not Zedekiah when he opposed Micaiah, nor Hananiah when he opposed Jeremiah, nor any other—who would be accounted false prophets. They would all be taken for true, and yet were deceivers; as Paul and Timothy here were accounted deceivers, and yet were true.

One especial reason given by good authors why Jonah should be so angry, and so very angry, that Nineveh was spared, was his own credit—that he might not be thought a false prophet, a deceiver, though he was true. Jeremiah also, when the princes would have put him to death as a false prophet, regarded not his life, but stood in defense of the truth he had spoken: "As for me, behold, I am in your hand: do with me as seemeth good and meet unto you. But know ye for certain, that, if ye put me to death, ye shall surely bring innocent blood upon yourselves, and upon this city, and upon the inhabitants thereof, for of a truth the Lord hath sent me unto you to speak all these words in your ears," (Jeremiah 26:14–15).

So, Paul often vindicates his credit, and stands upon his sincerity in preaching the Gospel: "For we are not as many, which corrupt the word of God, but as of sincerity, but as of God, in the sight of God speak we in Christ," (2 Corinthians 2:17). And again: "But have renounced the hidden things of dishonesty, not walking in craftiness, nor handling the word of God deceitfully; but by manifestation of the truth commending ourselves to every man's conscience in the sight of God," (2 Corinthians 4:2). And this is what every faithful minister of Jesus Christ should especially stand upon—for "Cursed be he that doeth the work of the Lord deceitfully," (Jeremiah 48:10)—that his words be the words of *truth and soberness*.

Let the world judge as it will of the manner of our preaching. Sometimes they say we are too hot, sometimes too cold; sometimes too learned, sometimes too unlearned; sometimes too high, sometimes too plain; sometimes too sharp, sometimes too pleasing. Let the world say what it will—if we speak the truth in Christ, our consciences bearing us witness in the Holy Spirit, the guide of our consciences, that we do not lie, keeping back nothing that is profitable to the people, but declaring to them the whole counsel of God—we may then find joy and comfort to our souls, when all the comforts of the world shall fail us.

And in this way, I have shown you what a minister of Jesus Christ may pass through. I shall now come to the second point, and show that it is the lot of many a dear servant of God to pass through them all.

And where should I begin to give an instance, if not with our crucified Lord? One day honored, when He rode into Jerusalem, with boughs and garments spread in the way, and the joyful shout of "Hosanna; Blessed is he that cometh in the name of the Lord; Hosanna in the highest," (Matthew 21:9). And the fifth day after, most shamefully dishonored, with the continuing cry of "Crucify him, crucify him" (Luke 23:21). In which death, as I said before, there may be doubt whether there was more pain or shame: pain enough to satisfy for our pleasures, and shame enough to satisfy for our pride.

That is for honor and dishonor. Now for His good report and evil report: Sometimes He was reported to be a prophet, a great prophet, a teacher come from God; that He was true, and taught the way of God in truth, and cared for no man, nor regarded the person of men; and lastly, that "He hath done all things well," (Mark 7:37). At other times, He was reported to be a blasphemer, an enemy to Caesar, a seducer of the people, a gluttonous man, a winebibber, a friend of publicans and sinners, a Samaritan, one who had a devil, one who wrought by Beelzebub the prince of devils. Would they not then call Him a deceiver too? Yes: while some said, "He is a good man," others said, "Nay; but he deceiveth the people," (John 7:12). And the chief priests and

Pharisees said plainly to Pilate, "Sir, we remember that that deceiver said, while he was yet alive, After three days I will rise again," (Matthew 27:63). And yet, though He was called a deceiver, He showed Himself true in that, for *praedixit et revixit*—He foretold it, and did it in His time.

But, holy brethren, to come to my third point, in which I will make the use of all this: we may prove ourselves to be the true ministers of Jesus Christ if neither honor puffs us up, nor dishonor disheartens us; if neither a good report makes us proud, nor an evil report makes us fainthearted, but we can pass through all these—honor and dishonor, evil report and good report—counting nothing in life, nor life itself dear to us, so long as we may finish our course with joy, and the ministry which we have received from the Lord Jesus Christ.

To that end, let me briefly tender these things to our *consideration:*

First, this change of honor and dishonor, evil report and good report, is from the Lord, who must be allowed to do what seems good in His eyes. The time was, we confess with thankfulness, when the people esteemed us as the ministers of Jesus Christ; when they knew us, acknowledged us worthy, and had us in exceeding great love, for our work's sake; when they showed they could have plucked out their eyes to have done us good, when they honored us with much honor, and loaded us with what was necessary, with plentiful provision for our encouragement in the ministry. Having received so much good at the hand of God, may we not now with patience receive some evil? There is no evil done in the city in this kind, but the Lord has done it (Amos 3:6). God has bidden them curse us, revile us, traduce us, and load us with all these reproaches. Yet, if these things are sanctified to us, God may do us good even through our reproaches. We should consider that, as they do not come without just desert—since God is just—so they will not pass away without profit, since God is good.

Consider again: there is nothing that can come from the hand of this God to His servants, but it comes in the nature of mercy. While we were honored, it was mercy to encourage us; now that we are dishonored, and our souls filled with contempt, it is mercy to admonish us to walk more humbly with God, and more carefully with men.

Again, it is only the pride of our hearts that makes us so impatient of every light dishonor; for if we were as we ought to be—vile in our own eyes—it would be nothing to be vile in the eyes of others. Besides, hear what our Lord says to His disciples: "Blessed are you when men shall say all manner of evil against you falsely for my sake; rejoice and be glad, for so they persecuted the prophets who were before you", (Matthew 5:11–12). The prophets, before the apostles, were so persecuted; the apostles, and all the worthies since their time, have been so persecuted in their several generations; and our blessed Lord, the head of both prophets and apostles, was, as you heard before, persecuted in like manner.

Now, the disciple must not expect to be above his master, nor the servant above his lord. It is enough for the disciple to be as his master, and the servant as his lord. If they have called the master of the house Beelzebub, how much more will they call those of his household? (Matthew 10:24–25).

Lastly, behold, there is a crown in the right hand of Christ, and the word upon it is, "To him that overcomes." Brethren, let us hold fast what we have, and let no man take away our crown. Let us *continue* to divide the Word of God rightly, and to walk with a right foot in the profession of it; to act innocently, and to preach wisely—not studying so much to have our gifts commended, as to have God glorified, consciences edified, lives reformed, and souls saved. And then, if we find favor in God's sight, He may bring us again into favor with men; but if He says, "I have no delight in you, nor in your services," behold, here we are—let Him do with us as He pleases.

He that, passing through honor and dishonor, as St. Paul did, can say as St. Paul said, I have fought the good fight, I have finished my course, I have kept the faith—I have kept it—may be assured of a crown of righteousness laid up for him, which the Lord, the righteous Judge, shall give him on that day, and to all those who love the appearing of our Lord Jesus Christ. To whom, with the Father and the blessed Spirit, three persons, one true, immortal, invisible, only wise God, be given all honor, glory, dominion, and power, now and forever. Amen.

Other Works at Puritan Publications on Worship

5 Marks of a Biblical Church by C. Matthew McMahon

5 Marks of Biblical Commitment to the Visible Body of Christ by C. Matthew McMahon

A Biblical Response to Superstition, Will-Worship and the Christmas Holiday by Daniel Cawdrey (1588-1664)

A Christian's True Spiritual Worship to Jesus Christ by Stephen Charnock (1628-1680)

A Declaration of the Christian Sabbath by Robert Cleaver (d. 1613)

A Discourse on Church Discipline and Reformation by Daniel Cawdrey (1588-1664)

A Discourse on Covenant Theology and Infant Baptism by Cuthbert Sydenham (or Sidenham) (1622–1654)

A Discourse on Self-Examination by Nathaniel Vincent (1639-1697)

A Gospel-Ordinance Concerning the Singing of Scripture Psalms, Hymns and Spiritual Songs by Cuthbert Sydenham (1622–1654)

A Practical Guide to Primeval History by C. Matthew McMahon

A Treatise on the Lord's Supper by Henry Smith (1550–1591)

A Watchman Over Christ's Church by C. Matthew McMahon

Attending the Lord's Table by Henry Tozer (1602-1650)

Bah Humbug: How Christians Should Think About the Christmas Holiday by C. Matthew McMahon

Christ's Directives on the Nature of True Worship by Arthur Hildersham (1563-1631)

Christian Truths Necessary for Salvation by Nicholas Byfield (1579–1622)

Covenant Holiness and Infant Baptism by Thomas Blake (1597-1657)

Directions for Daily Holy Living by Daniel Burgess (1645-1713)

Family Reformation Promoted, and Other Works by Daniel Cawdrey (1588-1664)

Gospel Music: or the Singing of David's Psalms by Nathaniel Holmes (or Homes) D.D. (1599–1678)

Gospel Worship, or, The Right Manner of Sanctifying the name of God in General, in Hearing the Word, Receiving the Lord's Supper, and Prayer by Jeremiah Burroughs (1599-1646)

How to Hear the Preaching of God's Word with Profit by Stephen Egerton (1555–1621)

How to Serve God in Private and Public Worship by John Jackson (1600-1648)

Infant Baptism God's Ordinance by Michael Harrison (1640-1729)

Infant Baptism of Christ's Appointment by Samuel Petto (1624–1711)

Love to God by Thomas Tuke (d. 1657)

Practical Observations on the Lord's Supper by C. Matthew McMahon

Presumptive Regeneration, or, the Baptismal Regeneration of Elect Infants by Cornelius Burgess (1589-1665)

Singing of Psalms a Gospel Ordinance by John Cotton (1585-1662)

Singing of Psalms the Duty of Christians by Thomas Ford (1598–1674)

Sparks of Divine Glory: A Practical Study of the Attributes of God by C. Matthew McMahon

The Christian's Charge Never to Offend God in Worship by John Forbes (1568-1634)

The Christian's Duty to Reject Christmas by Thomas Mockett (or Mocket) (1602-1670)

The Cursed Family, or the Evil of Neglecting Family Prayer by Thomas Risley (1630–1716)

The Difficulties of and Encouragements to a Reformation by Anthony Burgess (1600-1663) and C. Matthew McMahon

The Doctrine and Practice of Infant Baptism by John Brinsley (1600-1665)

The Excellent Name of God by Jeremiah Burroughs (1599-1646)

The Glory of Evangelical Worship by John Owen (1616-1683)

The Guard of the Tree of Life, a Discourse on the Sacraments by Samuel Bolton (1606-1654)

The Holy Eucharist, or, the Mystery of the Lord's Supper Briefly Explained by Thomas Watson (1620-1686)

The Lord's Voice Cries to the City: A Biblical Guide for Hearing the Word of God Preached by C. Matthew McMahon

The Nature and Method of Secret Prayer by Samuel Lee (1625-1691)

The Preacher's Charge and People's Duty by John Brinsley (1600-1665)

The Puritans on Exclusive Psalmody Edited by C. Matthew McMahon

The Simplicity of Holy Worship by John Wilson (1588–1667)

The True Psalmody by Various Reformed Ministers

The Use of Instruments of Music in Christian Corporate Worship Indefensible by James Begg, D.D.

True Worship and the Consequences of Idolatry by John Knox (1505-1572)

Vain Imaginations in the Worship of God by Jonathan Edwards et al.

www.ingramcontent.com/pod-product-compliance
Lightning Source LLC
LaVergne TN
LVHW091149080826
845145LV00008B/2311

* 9 7 8 1 6 2 6 6 3 5 3 7 1 *